ACCOUNTABILITY IN AN UNACCOUNTABLE WORLD

Matthew Brandt
the Accountability Cop

TIFFANY
ENJOY!

TABLE OF CONTENTS

PREFACE

As a young boy growing up in Oregon, I vividly remember hearing my parents telling incredible stories of men like General Patton, Admiral Nimitz, President's Eisenhower and Kennedy. Certainly, they were war-time heroes during that time frame of American history; some obvious national leadership successes as well. This country's fight for international democracy created enormous opportunity, though no guarantee, for such men to emerge on the world's stage as powerful, dedicated leaders. Though each had a unique method and brand of leadership, they understood what global accountability meant.

My father was a World War II era veteran, and a United States Marine, and eventually a career law enforcement officer. He had his opinion about these men who stepped up to the challenge at a time when it was most certainly needed. Those men came through their own battles; be it in the jungles of the Pacific or within the beltway of Washington. He grew up through the ranks and ultimately understood what successful leadership looked like at that time.

Though he didn't speak very often about his time in the Pacific, his time and service, was incredible to say the least. It took place in some very difficult parts of the world. After his departure from San Diego, he first landed for a short time on the island of Tinian in the Northern Marianas. From there it was the move to the island of Pavuvu; headquarters to the Marine 1st Division, only recently relocated up from Australia. Then it was on to wading ashore, April 1st, 1945 on the island of Okinawa. He later became a China Marine and helped liberate China from its war time occupation. I'm proud of my father's service and sorry for what he had to see and endure.

I later found out, most ironically that I would find myself also visiting the island of Okinawa on April 1st, 1985. Forty years to the day that my father waded ashore; I too arrived at White Beach aboard a U.S. warship carrying about 1,000 U.S. Marines. It was probably that day that I realized how, in a global sense, leadership and accountability weighed heavy on so many people, throughout history.

In his later years, he did sit down with me and explained everything that took place during his time with the Marine Corps in the Pacific. He talked specifically about many of the leaders that he followed on to landing crafts and into the jungles. Some, he said, were extremely good leaders as we have all grown to know and remember (mainly because of Hollywood) as well as our recent actions in the middle east these past several years. But he also said very clearly, that he followed many people that were placed into leadership roles at that point in the war where they had no business being there. For their safety and that of all the men to the left and right of him.

Young officers entering the ranks from many walks of life, often with drastically shortened training periods needed to learn combat leadership. It's one thing to fail in how we train leaders in the corporate world today,but not when real lives most certainly will depend on their decisions. Can this happen anytime and at any point in our country's history? Yes, of course it can. However, as we create and grow new leaders today, we need to do our very best to ensure we not only give them the tools they need to learn, but the opportunity to practice them, before the ramp on the landing craft falls onto the beach; and real men and women's lives are on the line.

Success during that time, was often measured simply by accomplishing some basic goals they set out to achieve on any given day.

Ensuring they had the resources available, where and when they were needed, and leading people who otherwise were not accustomed to being led, to do something that in most cases they didn't or wouldn't want to do otherwise. One question I asked my father was; how did they do it? How did the Marine Corps teach 19-year old boys to lead men into battle?

The answer was always the same; "they taught accountability." Accountability in the sense of how they shaped behavior, how they learned team-work and how leaders led; from the front. Accountability was about behavior not punishment. In 1945, accountability was a highlight of leadership training. So how have we allowed global leadership failures to be the leading cause of why people leave their jobs today? Why did we let this happen?

I'm grateful for the lessons my father learned, as tough as they may have been. Because of him, I learned some very critical lessons. It has given me the ability to successfully lead men and women in law enforcement, on the streets of America today.

For those who can neither remember those times, nor have heard the stories of what it took to be a leader then, it was far more than merely higher profit margins or producing more widgets than the next company. Success at any time in history may even be merely maintaining the organization exactly as it has been for the last decade, so as not to upset the apple cart of the corporate structure. Maintaining the status quo was often how a company won.

Time, technology and the lack of real-world crisis experience has depleted our ability to learn real leadership. We have become a globally unaccountable leadership workforce, in my opinion.

As a country of innovators, creators, organizers and leaders I think we've lost a step or two on improving upon the lessons of prior generations.

In reality; today's leadership training should incorporate the lessons learned from history, wherever the best lessons may have very well come from. World history, and the issues that we are faced with today, are the same issues faced 50 or 100 years ago. Setting out with specific goals that defines success in what we do and have the necessary resources in place. Whether it's people or infrastructure to carry out those goals, while most importantly, holding the organization accountable (the people) for their actions and behaviors as we move forward toward that goal.

Where leaders fall short today, is in the reliance of technology as a replacement for human leadership. Technology has allowed us to improve the speed by which we do things and even maybe the accuracy. It has also improved the techniques by which we accomplish some tasks, and it certainly has improved our communication opportunities.

But the positive direction technology created, also has left a vacuum of accountability and leadership in the wake. I believe the likes of Patton, Nimitz, Kennedy and especially Reagan; the great communicator would probably find this offensive.

Life in the workplace or battlefield is very different today. We see dozens of books, articles and news reports on the various generations. Millennials, Generation X or Generation Y issues that have become what I believe is the crutch of the very people raised during those times. Today it's easy to say "ah, he's a Gen X'er what do you expect?

What I expect is for him to step up to the plate and do what he is paid to do and stop falling back on what his perception of what he believes the world owes him.

Are you able to imagine a platoon of Generation X soldiers in Patton's march across Africa? What about a ship full of Millennial Sailors and Marines at Iwo Jima or Okinawa?

I know we have very capable troops serving today, however I struggle as I watch today's leaders fail over and over. Is that the fault of technology or leadership allowing it to happen? Maybe both.

The technology revolution has seen greater success in our modern world than this nation saw during than any other time in modern history.

The advances made in the past 30 years have out maneuvered every aspect of life, far out weighing what our grandparents and great-grandparents experienced in their youth.

With that however comes a side to leadership that was simply not expected nor handled appropriately as everyone was caught up in the waves of technology.

Pagers, Blackberries, Iphones, e-mail and video conferencing have replaced one-on-one communication, hand-written notes, correspondence and real-time communication. Speed is everything; increased productivity means more sales, more exposure, more revenue, and a higher bottom line.

However, the one thing technology has failed to figure out, is how to increase time itself. We have become so dependent on accomplishing more, creating more, more widgets, attending more meetings that we have come to a point of saturation in many arenas. Again, is this a leadership issue that must be addressed through accountability or is it something else?

Corporate leaders, military leaders and leaders of industry as well as every level of supervision below them have such innate pressure to accomplish more, with less. Be more places, attend more meetings, approve more programs, create new ideas, sell more products that the "traditional" 8-hour day has turned into the 12 to14-hour day in many organizations. Where is this taking us? Isn't technology supposed to make our lives easier, more accommodating, free-up time? Where it's taking us is to the brink of imploding on our own technological success, while watching our leadership skills fall by the wayside.

Line level workers are looking around wondering where their organization is heading because all they hear are the rumors from everyone except his or her own leadership. Mid-level managers have their eyes set on the next big idea or product and have lost the ability to communicate with those whom carry out the day-to-day business of making their organizations work. They have simply lost touch from where they began.

Senior level leaders have lost the ability to lead as a result of coming up through those very ranks, learning exactly what leadership training is being taught along the way, very little.

Do more with less, work longer and faster using technology, and get a piece of the pie before the ceiling crumbles. Well don't look now, everything seen falling isn't merely rain, it may be pieces of the ceiling.

The ability to communicate through the human bond of one-on-one conversations is becoming a lost art. Much like the use of cursive handwriting is quickly becoming a thing of the past in the teachings and use of our children; it's quickly giving way to texting and e-mails.

As leaders it is easy to ignore e-mails and it's easy to have administrative staff take messages for you, but what is difficult, is to look someone in the eye and give solid constructive criticism, counseling on potential improvements in their work product or even show praise for a job well done. It's not that leaders can't do it, anyone can do it, but it has become so comfortable to hide behind the wall of technology and lead by e-mail that the following generations are in serious trouble.

If we fail to pass on the ability to act as a true leader as it was meant to be and as history has shown was most successful; will this nation ever find its next Patton, Nimitz, or Kennedy? Being accountable in an unaccountable world is where we are left today.

We come full circle and the question is; where have all the leaders gone? The simple answer is, nowhere.

They have worked hard at developing leadership skills through formal education and incremental experience; through a gradual rise within organizations. Those leaders that are gaining supervisory experience at a basic line level, and the responsibility that accompanies it are the next true leaders of today.

What is missing in our senior most leaders today is a specific skill set. A skill set that impresses upon leaders to personally interact with those whom they rely on to move the organization forward. Entrust in the fact that human contact, creating personal relationships with employees, supervisors, stakeholders and even the competition creates a wealth of knowledge and trust in the ability to lead, especially when times are difficult.

Leading during the good times is easy; everyone will follow a leader to paradise without much prodding. But when the organization turns toward a battlefield, look around, and see who is still following. Creating those interpersonal relationships with subordinates, other leaders and stakeholders creates a certain trust and bond that cannot be interpreted or easily digested by an outgoing e-mail.

Make time to simply stop by and say "hello" to the new guy on the assembly line, gain his trust today and he'll stick with you for years to come, in good times, and bad.

Remember to lead as history has shown us is most successful, from the front. Then set goals and hold people accountable by changing poor behavior into positive action.

Don't get caught leading from behind the wall of technology. Where have all the leaders gone? They are right here; reading, learning, better understanding history as well as lessons learned by those doing the job today.

Being accountable in an unaccountable world today is possible. You are taking a step today by reading and learning from someone that has fought the fight and has learned a few hard lessons.

Welcome aboard!

CHAPTER 1

LESSONS LEARNED

Figure 1. *Descending from the private residence of the President*

P icture this…. it's February 28th, 1984, I'm a Navy Sailor standing proud at 6'4" in my dress blue uniform…. On this night, I am the personal escort to the First Lady of the United States; Nancy Reagan. I'm standing motionless and disciplined in the East Room of the White House. Standing next to me is President Kirchschlaeger and his wife, the first lady of the Republic of Austria. Next to them is the 40th President of the United States, Ronald Reagan and his wife, the First Lady Nancy Reagan.

The receiving line stretched around the entire East Room from the left. I saw in my peripheral vision as people started to move and the Reagans and Kirchschlaegers began to receive invited guests. Olympic Champion Dorothy Hamill, Mega-star actor Larry Hagman, actress Patricia Neal and many, many more. One after another they filed around the East Room to meet the Presidents and First Ladies before dinner was served on this most auspicious evening; a formal White House State Dinner.

Black tie tuxedos, long beautiful evening gowns, the fanfare was as pristine and as elegant as anything or any place I'd ever seen. As a young man, having grown up in Grants Pass, Oregon, that level of grace and elegance was nothing like anything I'd ever experienced before. I was watching history unfold before my eyes and to think, I was taking part in that historical evening in our nation's White House!

As the receiving line continued to cycle through and one actor, athlete, admiral and general after another filed past me, I became more and more relaxed and settled in to my job that night. I was representing the entire United States Navy to world that evening and doing so in a very professional way. That was all well until the likes of two comedians; Phyllis Diller and Dom Deluise stepped in front of me.

These two were bigger than life during that time. Both were now staring directly at me, intently, stoic faces, as if to look deep into my eyes.

That I later learned was the set-up, as they simultaneously let out a belly laugh and scream, complete with contorted faces that only those two comedians could do without any sense of premonition.

At first it startled me, then as Ms. Diller reached out and pulled my uniform neckerchief tight up around my neck, I knew I had been targeted by this comedic team. My eyes began to water, I was biting my tongue so hard it was bleeding. "Do not laugh" I told myself! I momentarily closed my eyes and tried to distance myself from that time and place. The discipline of the Navy Ceremonial Guard, the history of all the Navy now rested on my shoulders as the crowd watched to see if I would crack; to see if I would buckle at the hands of these two bigger than life comedians.

Just as I was about to succumb to what was quickly becoming the focal point of everyone in the White House that night... I heard the President over my left shoulder say, as only he could, and as any husband or father would say just before something happened. The 40th President said; "Ooooh no....." As your grandfather might say under his breath in church just before you finger snapped your sister on the ear.

The room began to quiet down a bit; I opened my eyes to see what was happening. Nancy Reagan, the First Lady of the United States stepped directly in from of me with her index finger raised, like any mother correcting a child for misbehaving. "Not tonight, not in the White House" she said to both Diller and Deluise, looking directly at them like any motherly figure, like my mother, like your mother.... "Not tonight, not in the White House."

Figure 2. *Receiving line, East Room of the White House*

I will forever remember that moment. The two comedians immediately went silent; their faces went from hysterical laughter to solemn and nondescript. The room was now quiet as a whisper.

All the laughter had drained out of them and they knew they had stepped over the line right then and there.

The First Lady turned around and stepped up close to me, like a mother fixing her son's jacket before his wedding, or a young boy before going into church. She pulled my necktie back down to its proper place, straightened my uniform a bit at the shoulders, stepped back to look at me. She then leaned in and whispered to me, so only I could hear; "Not tonight, not in the White House." Ensuring once again that my uniform was proper, and that I again was distinguished and able to continue doing my job that night.

Diller and Deluise both said a rebuffed quiet apology to the First Lady and continued down the line. I never saw either again.

As a young man, standing there in the East Room of the White House I watched as the First Lady took a stand for what was right.

She was the smallest person in that room that night; 100 lbs. soaking wet, but she stood taller than anyone else. She knew and truly understood what later would become my three A's of leadership. Authority=Action=Accountability.

I stood there until every guest had passed the receiving line and we moved to the White House Dining Room to continue the very scripted evening. Speeches and toasts by President Reagan, then President Kirchschlaeger; followed by an evening of entertainment at the hands of pianist Peter Nero and jazz singer Mel Torme kept the evening enjoyable and as the First Lady had hoped, proper and distinguished as the White House had demanded.

As I stood, in back of the White House Dining Room that night, watching this historical event, I just could not shake what had happened earlier in the evening. "The First Lady of the United States had stepped in on my behalf" kept running through my head.

She did so when I could not because of military discipline and protocol, but it was more than that. She had stepped in as a leader to all of us that night. As not only the wife of our President, as the First Lady of the United States, but as America's leading mother; she was holding accountable or changing the behavior of two of the most popular and highly regarded celebrities in our country that night.

I saw first-hand that accountability was about changing behavior and not punishment or discipline.

She knew this was her home and it was her place to ensure those that were there as her guests, acted and responded in a way that she desired, and demanded. In front of two presidents, multiple cabinet members, Members of Congress, and countless celebrities. She had the authority, she took action, and changed their behavior. Lesson learned!

It was a profound evening that would shape how I would later lead during not only my Navy career but also how I would lead the men and women of law enforcement at a time when our country needed to not fail. In a time after September 11th, 2001 as we built an organization from the ground up, it was the lessons learned far earlier, in the East Room of the White House that I reflected on and passed along to every young supervisor I could.

Have you ever thought that somewhere, at some place, at some-time…we lost the true understanding of accountability in our lives? Ya…me too. I think many Americans and even other societies and countries have the same feeling every now and then. We are in a different place and different time today and many of the societal norms most of us grew up with or seemingly just knew and understood, are fading away.

What about the organization you work in? The employees you lead? How about the leaders above you?

We can look in any direction of our lives, from our home to the companies we work for, or the teams we lead, that accountability or the ability to change poor behavior into positive action is becoming a lost art today.

My nearly three years spent working next to the President and First Lady were some of the most exciting times of my life.

Not only because I was able to spend many days supporting them, but it allowed me to listen, learn and absorb, from whom at the time, were two of the most interesting and powerful "teachers" in the world.

Accountability as we understand it or seem to understand it is about discipline and punishment when something or someone fails to meet the expectations. At least that was my understanding of the word until that night.

Holding someone accountable for something meant if they didn't do the task, they got in trouble! At least in my young military career I could attest to that train of thought, so I thought.

I had just joined the U.S. Navy and had undergone basic training in San Diego, California. That place and time set aside to change young men and women, from reckless, undisciplined civilians into a fine tuned, well trained, team oriented young Sailors. What I learned there was; if you do bad things, make bad decisions, you do a lot of push-ups. Do good things, listen and learn, well....you still do push-ups. Although in the end listening, learning, growing together as a team earned you far fewer push-ups. But the fact remained, everyone did push-ups! However, change behavior they did that long hot summer in San Diego.

That evening in the East Room of the White House, as a young-man, I learned for the first time that accountability was meant to change behavior.... whatever the behavior, for whatever the reason.

When someone displays behavior that is not in line with your expectations, the organizations, the CEO, a written policy, performance plans or that of the First Lady of the United States.

Whatever device used to measure the required actions of a person.... Accountability is really about modifying behavior. Not punishment! Oh how I wish my Navy Drill Instructors could have learned that lesson!

When the 1st Lady stepped in front of me, in front of hundreds of people, in front of the visiting President and his wife.... And said: "not tonight, not in the White House." Nancy Reagan was speaking for all of America that night. She was teaching all of us a lesson about leadership, accountability and behavioral change.

Do you have the same moxie that Nancy Reagan had that night? Do your other supervisors, managers and senior leaders have it?

It's been more than 30 years since we all had the pleasure of watching President Reagan and his wife Nancy, grace the nation with everything they did. He; The Great Communicator and she his loyal and trusted partner of many years. Whether you are a fan of the Reagans or not, whether you were even alive at the time they led this nation, I can tell you they were old-school patriots, with old-school manners and actions. Can we learn from them today? Probably.

You are asking yourself why does all this matter to you? You picked up this book to learn how to hold people accountable and how to improve leadership skill set. How to improve your team, your organization maybe even your kids! Yes your kids! Getting your own kids to clean their room, take out the garbage, mow the lawn, do the dishes, the countless things we ask our children to do every day as part of the family and keeping a reasonably kept home. Could it work on them? Really?

What can a young Navy Sailor working at the White House learn and teach me today? In this millennial and Gen Z led workforce, where so it seems that accountability is more like a foreign word than a way of life?

In the 1980's, together, the Reagans changed the behavior of this nation.

They even changed the behavior of many of our partner countries around the globe. How did they do that?How did they pick this nation up by the boot straps and give all of us a sense of ownership in our country, buy-in to the belief that we were bigger than any one-person or one thing?

In the 1980's the Reagan White House had us all believing in ourselves, believing in our country, believing in the notion of "Accountability."

Remember in 1981 when the Air Traffic Controllers went on strike? The President fired 11,000 federal employees in one-day! Why? He was holding them accountable to the orders of the President to return to work. Think about the magnitude of that action.....11,000 workers! He was truly only trying to change behavior in those workers, and they refused. At that point, they were no longer useful to the results he wanted. He tried to change their behavior and gave them a much needed "out" that allowed them to win the day should they have chosen to, yet we know the story and they didn't.

One of the fantastic things about working in the Reagan White House was listening and learning. Watching and modeling, what I would later learn was that President Reagan was well versed on accountability (otherwise why would I be writing this book!)

Below are a few quotes our 40th President said and or wrote during his time in the White House. They were true then and ring true still today. They are applicable in every organization and yes, family in America and even around the world.

President Reagan wrote this about his take on Accountability:

When our forefathers' declared independence from England, they sent a signal to the world that freedom and liberty are only possible when each person is allowed to determine how to live their life.

They called these God-given rights. And with these rights come responsibilities.

We teach our children they will be held accountable for their actions. We tell them they will reap what they sow. Yet they often see lawbreakers set free, or never arrested in the first place. Many who are sent to prison commit more crimes upon their release.

This cycle repeats itself time and time again until the laws cease to be a deterrent.

We must reject the idea that every time a law's broken, society is guilty rather than the lawbreaker. It is time to restore the American precept that each individual is accountable for his actions.

Personal responsibility is not a burden. It is a requirement for a country that was founded on the God-given rights of freedom and liberty.

To be truly free, one must be personally responsible.

Now, all is not lost today. In the almost 30 years I've spent in law enforcement and of that, more than 20 years in various leadership positions, it still pertains today. From a Patrol Officer to Patrol Sergeant and later Detective Sergeant, and now a senior leader with the U.S. Government, I've had the opportunity to see the worst in society, at all levels, including organizational unaccountability.

As a detective working robbery and homicides, child sex crimes and gangs, I've had the opportunity, I'll call it, to sit face to face, knee to knee, with some horrible people.

One man I remember had just killed his grandmother and really had no remorse about what he had done; he just kept asking if he could have a cigarette. No conscious, nothing.

I once interviewed a man that videotaped his sexual abuse of dozens of young boys over several years and he too, though he knew it was wrong, had no concept of human decency or remorse.

I mean these were bad people and I learned a great deal listening to them talk; listening to them explain in their minds, why they did what they did. It really helped me when I had to sit down and have hard conversations with failing employees who had trouble understanding what accountability was all about. One excuse ran into the other and the human nature of failing to be accountable for their actions sank in. People are people, know one and you know them all.

I know, you're asking yourself right now; how in the world is there any comparison to the minds of such horrible criminals and that of my employees, my boss or even my kids!

What I learned, was the thought process and reasoning behind both heinous criminal minds and any person today, is basically the same. People do what they do, even really good and well-intentioned people, because in their minds they believe it's normal, it's even....OK. Those employees that you have, even managers that do and say some bizarre things, also think it's normal and ok to ignore certain required behaviors or tasks they have at work. Human nature has shown that most supervisors or managers, even higher-level organizational leaders won't correct their behavior. They just don't!

If we don't learn a few basic and easily applied rules of the game, then people will, much like water, most often take the path of least resistance and avoid conflict. They will fail to act in hopes that whatever the problem, issue, project, chore, that somehow it will be forgotten or reassigned or more time will be given to do the work.

It's unfortunate, but humans are humans and until you dig a little deeper into what drives human behavior, you will forever be trying to correct behavior that is honestly human nature and part of our human DNA.

Please understand I'm not a psychologist nor do I formally study human behavior. However, after this long in a profession where nearly every single person I encountered would sit before me, crying, begging me to believe them…. yet lie to me repeatedly. With that, I've learned a few things about human behavior and what lessons we might take from these interactions. How to weave them into leadership moments and how accountability and the molding of behavior is very much attainable if you know a few simple rules.

The failure as I see it across most organizations, whether it's a Fortune 500 company, a non-profit, or the United States government is that we all fail to properly teach and train brand new supervisors how to lead. Simple as that…answer that question in any context you like, and I believe you will create generation after generation of successful CEO's, COO's and senior leaders in any organization, even the U.S. government!

Fail to do that, like we continue to fail today, and you will only perpetuate the never-ending rotation of mediocre, wishy washy first and second line supervisors. Whose egos out pace their abilities, and who in the end often, cost your organization thousands if not millions of dollars or more over time.

So much money is spent in hiring and training new employees over and over to replace employees those that had no real chance at success. All due to the failure of first line supervision and mentorship. The departure of personnel whose actions potentially could have been realigned, guided, molded into productive employees.

Money spent on attorney's defending bad decisions made by unskilled supervisors trying to slog the waters of labor law and fair labor standards.

These same people, some of them, make it through those early years, some with costly learning curves, some by the grace of God for their ability to ignore or dodge real supervisory work and leadership. Those same people now become your Vice-President of Sales, or your Chief Operating Officer, maybe the CEO or Senior Executive. Now, they are on the hook for masses of employees. Multiple teams, projects, programs and all that are high value, high cost to the organization. When they fail at that level, the outcome can be catastrophic to the entire organization. Have companies completely folded based on poor decisions made by senior leaders? You bet they have.

Remember a little company called Enron? They were the epitome of leaders going off the rail in a major fashion and taking the entire company down with them. How about Blackberry, they once were the status symbol of the handheld phone or personal device; but leaders there were often promoted based on tenure in lieu of skills and abilities to lead. How about the bookstore Borders? Leaders failing to lead, failing to act, failing to see the future and having the ability to manage their employees. Failing to create opportunities, grow and change behavior, see the future of their industry. I could go on all day, but I think you get where I'm going.

This book is not here for the quick fix. What I mean by that, is you probably won't be overly successful in changing a large group of your failing supervisors today. Those people you either inherited or hired yourself that are failing you today, every day. They are failing to lead, failing to hold employees accountable (changing behavior) to ensure the immortality of your organization and for them it's simply too late.

I'm not here to try and fix the masses of those leaders. You can often help change behavior in some of your leaders, but what I'm talking about is the long-term health and productivity of your organization. Looking ahead 5, 10, 20 years from now.

You have young employees (hopefully) that may eventually become fantastic leaders, but first they must learn how to supervise. They must first learn to slog through the swamp of supervision at the lower levels before we should ever begin to even think about promoting them to higher, more senior levels of the organization. A place where bad moves, poor judgment, failing decisions at that level, could literally collapse the company. Let's make sure they can supervise a team of five or ten employees before we give him or her the keys to the Caddy!

24

That's my purpose with this book. It's meant to address how someone first understands the authority they have been given as a supervisor. Then they must learn and understand how important action is to their new position. Taking action or not taking action, depending on the situation is imperative. Finally, accountability or understanding the absolute need to change behavior. This can be learned and executed at early levels of a career and can create a life-time of success. True leaders that you grow and cultivate from within your organization to lead the next generation on the lessons you and I have learned today.

"Not tonight, not in the White House"

-Nancy Reagan

CHAPTER 2

AUTHORITY

Authority

Everyone has it; be it a mother to her children, the custodian to the building he cleans, or a CEO to her organization....What so many people forget, is they were hired to do a job, some job, any job, and with that job comes some amount of innate authority to do that job. Simple right?

If you're a parent, you have a certain amount of authority over your children, it's an authority that only you as the parent has. If you're an accountant, you have some level of authority to manage the money, pay the bills, close invoices. If you're the supervisor of a team, you have a level of authority over that team to ensure they are doing the job they were hired to do. You also have a level of authority to act on behalf of the organization when times are not so good, as well as encouraging and commending your team, building confidence, morale and overall just taking care of your people. Knowing your given authority in the job you are in is the 1st key to being successful in that job. Highlight that, write it down, take that note. The first key to understanding leadership 101 is that you have a certain level of authority to lead, to act and to represent the bigger organization.

In this country, probably in most countries, we do a poor job teaching young, new supervisors what authorities they have in managing their new team. From progressive discipline, to awards and accommodations, we don't teach new supervisors ALL the authority they have at their hands.

This is how it happens most often. Someone in the company really has a talent at selling the company product or providing some service, building widgets, whatever it is your company does.

Maybe they are outspoken a little bit, probably have a little charisma in how they are perceived by others and are trusted by their peers and their leaders. They are often "good people" and great at what they do, today; here and now.

Now that is not always the case. We know plenty of people in our organizations that have been promoted for reasons far from being "good" at selling, fixing, servicing, or building the company widget. How often have we seen the person that has recently arrived at the company, maybe been known to the CEO or senior manager and suddenly becomes the golden child. He or she can't do anything wrong, maybe has the college degree amongst others that don't and have never needed one to be successful for decades in the company.

Today, someone just becomes the chosen one and is fast-tracked to management. A hundred different ways to be on this track, you know someone that passed you up that fits some form of this golden child persona.

Now, be it the golden child track to management or maybe the one that seems to have her head so far up the VP's back side he can barely walk; or a dozen others that have been promoted because they were "pretty good" at what they did while standing next to me at the bottom. It is likely that none of them will produce a successful next generation of leadership.

So what authority do you have in your job today? What are some of the types of authority I'm talking about when it comes to leaders and leadership positions? There are very legally mandating forms of authority.

As a police officer, I carry a certain level of authority given to me by the United States Congress.

I have the authority to make probable cause arrests, to carry firearms, to defend myself and others with deadly force. I can execute search and arrest warrants issued by legal authority (again, a type of authority) and a variety of other very legal sounding types of authority. So professionally, my authority to carry out my professional duties as a law enforcement officer, is given to me by Congress.

Doctors have a certain amount of professional authority in what they can and can't do in practicing medicine. Attorneys also have forms of authority to do certain things as prescribed by law. Teachers have the authority and requirement to report any type of suspected abuse of children. Accountants have certain authority given to them by their clients or the organization to receive and pay invoices, implement budgets, make and take out financial obligations and so on. These are just examples of some of the professional authorities that some people and their profession have. There are many more however and I can bet, that whatever your job is, you can back track and name a few. Even the most mundane or starter level jobs have some amount of "authority" to do something.

Let's say for instance you work as a shoe salesman in an average clothing store, anywhere in the world. Your job is to sell shoes, period. Men's shoes, women's shoes, kid's shoes; from athletic to pumps, loafers and high heels. The more you sell, the better the company does, the more profits it makes, and in the end the more commission maybe you make. You have the authority as a shoe salesman to restock penny loafers when they begin to sell out.

You have the authority to obligate company funds to purchase new penny loafers to restock the shelves of your shoe department. Does the person that cleans the department store bathroom have that authority? No, of course not. This is your department, you have that authority.

On the same shoe, but different foot (see even cops can tell a joke!) you as the shoe salesman don't have the authority to order new cleaning chemicals to wax the floors and scrub the toilets, that's simply not your authority to use. Are you tracking?

Every job has some form, often many forms of professional authority given to the position to carry out the actual function of that position. But what authority are you given in addition to that in-order to supervise all the other shoe salesmen? Is it the same authority or same "type" of authority? Do you know?

If you are hesitating right now as to what authority you have been given in your current job; you have a real problem. It doesn't matter if you are seeking a promotion to a supervisory position or if you're a seasoned leader in an organization. If you don't know what authority you have as a supervisor, manager or leader to carry out those management oversight duties then you won't know how to act and react when you should. Those critical moments when you need to know, need to act, can make or break your tenure as a competent leader. It can also cost your company tens of thousands of dollars in attorney fees and labor costs. If you don't know, learn!

As managers at any level, when we are selected to lead a group of people, we are given a vast amount of organizational authority to do that. Now in all fairness your company should tell you, teach you and mentor you in what those new authorities are when you are promoted. When you go from employee to supervisor; your learning curve should start all over.

The problem is, and I've already said it, one of the biggest issues we have in leadership today is most organizations fail at the basics of leadership training. There are a variety of leadership trainings and courses available that cover a wide range of big vision, global size leadership training. We teach young supervisors how to think like a CEO, but we don't do a very good job at teaching new supervisors, how to be new supervisors.

During my time as a young supervisor in the Navy, one of the best things, amongst many of the things I learned early on was that all the military service branches train their young non-commissioned officers how to supervise at the most basic level.

Since I'm a Navy guy, I'll speak to what the Navy did and continues to do today. I'm certain that all the other branches have very similar methods and may even do a better job. If only corporate America and for that matter, any corporation on the globe would do half as much, we'd see far fewer issues later in careers.

As you know I spent my first several years assigned to the White House. I was a member of the elite U.S. Navy Ceremonial Guard. Only 120 strong, we were a small but highly disciplined and well-trained group of professionals. We performed at not only White House state dinners, but a variety of White House ceremonies on the south lawn. We performed hundreds and hundreds of Navy funerals at Arlington National Cemetery and even on the Tomb of the Unknowns.

Military retirements, parades, special events and any place and time the Navy needed the best of the best as it related to ceremonies and Naval history; we were called to action.

Of the 120 assigned, we had maybe 10 supervisors. Most of whom did not come up through the ranks of the Ceremonial Guard. The working members of the Ceremonial Guard were a group of Sailors that were hand-picked directly from basic training graduates. We were the newest of the newest in the Navy.

As time progressed, each of us made our mark and at some point, either left the Navy or promoted up the ranks. To do so, required us to do several things before we could even be eligible to promote. That's an important step. Before you are even allowed to try or compete for promotion; you must learn the basics of supervision.

Can you imagine any company today putting on several layers of requirements to its line level employees, its line level shoe salesman to complete before they were even allowed to compete for promotion? Mind blown!

Now we can say that the Navy and other services have a great many people to "weed out" and ensure they never supervise even one person, so having these requirements in place before hand is merely a part of the selection process. Well, you're right it is!

Some people will never be able to get through those basic military requirements (BMRs or their first level of leadership requirements prior to competing for promotion, that is absolutely part of the process.

Some will get it done, and some will be given the opportunity to supervise others, while others will fail.

However, to succeed, means you have already proven to have at least some sense of basic knowledge as to what it takes to supervise others. From there it only becomes more difficult and more progressive the higher in rank you aim to achieve. Everyone that tries will reach a point of maximum ability. The Navy counts on that. I believe so should organizations today.

Let's back up a bit. In order to be given the opportunity to compete for a new supervisory position, how fantastic would it be if you had to pass a comprehensive training program and test of the basics in supervision? Once you pass that, you can now compete head-to-head with others that have passed it. Now as an organization you know, after the interview process, whomever is the best candidate already has a basic understanding of supervision 101. Already, you are way ahead of the power curve in breaking the ongoing and perpetual failure of supervisors knowing what authority they have and how to use it. What does your company use to prepare your line employees for their first supervisory job? Not to worry, you are taking fundamental steps here to learn some very important rules in your leadership tool belt.

Now, as a young Navy supervisor, a first line non-commissioned officer we call Petty Officer Third Class; you are normally given limited oversight of small groups of younger, lower ranking Sailors. You aren't given total oversight and management of them, but limited exposure to allow you ease into your new authority and allow your senior managers to observe, mentor and help guide you through those early supervision moments.

They really are moments of supervision. How great would that be in the corporate world?

Instead of being promoted and assigned a "team" or a "group" of employees to manage and lead from start to finish; new Third-Class Petty Officers can break in on small special details, short projects like cleaning crews, maintenance crews and such. It may be a 30-minute cleanup of the galley with four young Sailors assigned, to a day(s) maintenance of a piece of equipment that requires some technical expertise to complete. These short incremental stints as a supervisor are not make or break leadership roles.

They do however provide new young leaders with time and opportunity to learn how to motivate teams, how to overcome problems, how to handle communications and interpersonal relationships between people. The more they do, the more opportunities they will be given and the greater authority and responsibility they will be given.

Now, after some time, these young supervisors are ready for more and more authority and responsibility. Once again, they must read, study and take the next level of supervision course for Petty Officer Second Class. A higher rank, with more authority. Again, after they complete this basic course of study, they have earned the right to compete head-to-head with others that have also completed this next level of intermediate supervisory level. After being selected and promoted the entire process is started over again. This time however, more and more authority, responsibility and people are put under their leadership. Longer details, more Sailors and the learning process continues.

This step by step gradual learning of basic, intermediate and advanced supervisor and leadership concepts continue seven more times in your Navy career.

That's seven opportunities to learn more, to practice more and at any time you reach your maximum level of "ability" the Navy will simply stop your promotion ability. It rarely will put anyone in a position to lead others at a level they are not able to handle with extreme success. Now not always, there are one-offs of course, but it's rare.

You can see how this process though slow, produces supervisors that know how to supervise people, overcome problems, and will eventually become great senior leaders. At some point along a person's career they (and those leaders above them) will realize that a Sailor has reached a level of leadership competence that is all they can handle. For some that comes very early in their career and for others they continue to stretch and grow exponentially.

The authority that I've talked about here in my Navy example is not necessarily professional authority. The professional authority given to a member of the U.S. armed forces is to protect and defend the Constitution against all enemies, foreign and domestic. Pretty broad, fairly-wide ranging and having little to do with cleaning up the kitchen on a ship.

However, the authority that is spoon fed to those new supervisors (the Third-Class Petty Officer) in small bites, to use and learn from, is very effective and easily teachable and extremely learnable as a leader.

Let's compare that to today's corporate training program of new supervisors. Yesterday you were selling shoes on the department store floor. Today you are assigned the afternoon shift of six other shoe salesmen.

You will be given an increase in pay and expected to manage those six employees. Good luck! make sure you always meet your sales goals and keep the shelves stocked.

All goes well the first week. Your former peers and friends are happy you were selected as the new supervisor and you all basically continue along as you have for the months or years before. Then comes that day when one of your employees begins to take advantage of your long-term friendship prior to your new position. Coming in late like it was not a big deal, dressing unprofessionally, and even missing entire shifts. The other employees notice, now they are looking at you for how you will respond.

Are you ready for these decisions? Do you know what authority you must have to handle this issue? Do you know the legalities you are entering in by certain actions taken or not taken? Again, if you are asking yourself right now, what authority do I have? You have problems. These are answers to questions you should already know at this point in your supervisory job. If you don't, go find out!

As time goes on you continue to ignore this problem. The employee, thinking that you are his friend from the good ole days of selling penny loafers on the night shift, suddenly is called into YOUR supervisor's office and terminated. You then are called in and questioned as to why your team is failing? Why are the sales numbers falling? Why aren't people showing up for their shift on time, and why are you failing to take any action to correct these behaviors? All great questions and all understandable for your mid-level manager to ask you.

One or two things can happen at this point in your career as a newer supervisor. One, you wake up and realize you have no idea what you are doing as a supervisor.

You might realize you truly don't know or understand what authority you have in your new position nor how to use that new authority.

Second, your mid-level supervisor, the one above you, also has no idea about what authority he/she has, or what authority you have at your level and or even how-to mentor, or train you. He then tells you to do better next time, and off you go back to "lead" the remaining five shoe salesmen.

You manage to survive the next several months with your five shoe salesmen and suddenly your mid-level manager is fired (we can only imagine why) and you are pretty much automatically promoted to fill his position. More shifts to manage, more people to be responsible for and more authority given to you by the organization to carry out your new bigger role.

Now instead of the five people, you have 25 people over a variety of different shifts and several more pieces to manage. Schedules, payroll, the entire shoe department budget to manage as well as hiring authority to fill vacant positions to name a few. Remember you still have no more training than the day you arrived to sell your first pair of shoes. The only thing that has changed is your level of authority and responsibility. How are you feeling today? At first you feel pretty good. Successful career is moving along well, a little bump in pay, you're now a manager at the department store. Feel pretty good huh?

Let's go back to the first key in leadership 101. Understanding what authority, you do have in your position as a supervisor, manager or leader is still the 1st key to successfully leading others. A clueless leader is a worthless leader. A leader that is constantly knocking on the office door of his or her next level supervisor to ask; what should I do here?

What do you think about this? How should I proceed with this problem? It goes on and on.

If you're a mid-level manager or senior leader right now, you know exactly what I'm referring to. There is always at least one person (hopefully only one) but most likely many that continually fill your door way hour after hour, day after day with questions about how to supervise at the basic level. Don't be that person!

I've always been of the mindset, even when I wasn't sure about a decision I had to make or a direction to go in; just make a decision. Part of that little extra you receive in your paycheck is for making decisions. Young supervisors and even many newer mid-level managers will make plenty of mistakes. That's alright, most of those mistakes are part of the learning process of being a newer leader. Make them when you are new at the supervision game and hopefully you won't make them when you are the CEO where such a poor decision can literally ruin the company.

What was the 1st key to successful leadership? Right, authority!! If I had told you in the title of this book that the number one key to being successful as a leader was knowing your given authority, you never would have read another word. Like any job, supervision is as complicated and diverse in technical know how as any job in the world.

You must study it, you must practice it and it is one piece of any profession that you can never stop learning. From leading the shoe department in a department store, to the CEO of a Fortune 100 company, the rules are all the same. Knowing your authority to act in the leadership position you are currently is remains key #1.

"A clueless leader is a worthless leader"

-Matthew Brandt

CHAPTER 3

ACTION

If authority is key #1, you must assume there is a #2 coming right? You can see from our triangle, we are building upwards from Authority. Next is Action along the left angle. See you are already on your way to becoming a perceptive leader! From the title of this chapter it is no surprise that we are going to spend some time discovering the need for the action a supervisor must take while leading others.

This entire book, remember, is grounded based on the three principles all being equal. **Authority=Action=Accountability** is much like a quadratic equation. Without all three parts, you can never have a whole. Thus, the equal sign inside the equation. A leader that has been given the authority to supervise, manage or lead others we now know, has the backing of some entity. Maybe a policy or authoritarian body of some kind to use their authority to manage your team. That is all well and good, and of course very necessary. Action, however, is the means by which everything is accomplished.

Without action, it's just about the words on the paper or the thoughts of someone to get something done.

There are two parts to Action, taking it and failing to take it. Depending on the circumstances, the chosen route will determine whether the outcome is successful or failing. There are times when a leader should not take any action and simply let things play out before them. Now the ability to recognize that is an advanced level of leadership, but it's a lesson well learned.

Many people at all levels of an organization talk a lot about the necessary action that often needs to be taken, but few feel comfortable taking it. We call those people passive aggressive personalities, they are rampant in today's workforce.

Many like to talk the big game, but when it comes to taking action on the authority they've been given, they quickly fall apart. Not to worry really, it's part of our DNA. It's part of what makes us human.

This goes back, way back to the start of humanity. Now, just as I'm not psychologist, I'm not a human anthropologist either. I can tell you though that part of DNA, human DNA I mean, revolves around the survivability of our species. We know when we are hungry that we have to eat. Our body tells us that. Our brain is well programmed to send signals to us to find something to eat and nourish the needs of our body. We know when something is so hot it will hurt our bodies, so not to touch it. We know when it gets so cold out, our body again signals us by shivering (shaking muscles to try and warm itself) to find warmth.

Our human instincts tell us that we need to reproduce, so after puberty hits us, we are programmed to do just that. It's simply part of what makes a human being.

If you have not heard of the fight or flight response of the human body, let me quickly tell you now. Again, as part of our human make up, our brains are wired to be self-preserving. When humans are confronted with any form of fear, our hypothalamus, which is located directly in the middle of our brains, activates two systems simultaneously. The adrenal-cortical system and the sympathetic nervous system. The combined effect of these two systems are what most of know as the fight or flight response. When confronted with stress, like a supervisor needing to sit down with a problematic employee and have a difficult conversation about their performance, the hypothalamus kicks in automatically.

It will start the "fight or flight" response. The body thinks it needs to preserve itself, so it prepares to do just that.

The hypothalamus tells the sympathetic nervous system to kick into gear. The body speeds up, tenses up and becomes generally more alert. Signals are sent out to your glands and the smooth muscles; all while your adrenal gland is signaled to release the hormone epinephrine and noradrenaline into your bloodstream. These hormones cause both your heart rate and blood pressure to increase. Your pupils dilate to take in more light, veins in your skin constrict to send more blood to the major muscle groups and your blood-glucose levels increase. There is more, but you get where I'm going with this. Your body is ready to fight!

So just as when you are confronted with a burglar in your house in the middle of the night, your body reacts in similar fashion when you must confront a subordinate employee about an uncomfortable situation. Most people want to flee at this point vice fight, but your body knows no difference.

Here in lies the problem with this very human response. As a supervisor, it is dependent upon you to be the eyes, ears and voice of the organization. You are the first line of supervision which means you are the key to the largest part of the workforce every day. The greatest number of any company's employees, the heart of the workforce, is supervised by the first-line supervisor. If that is you, there is tremendous pressure on you to be successful in how you oversee this team. Remember our shoe salesman in chapter two? It didn't take us long to realize he was not prepared to be a successful first line supervisor.

It appeared in that example that he was never given any direction about his authority to lead, and as such, was not equipped to ever take any action when the time came. The time will always come, I assure you.

Overcoming the inability to take some form of action requires experience, courage, knowledge and first and foremost; the authority. Action without authority is a disaster in the making. Now that we know why the body reacts the way it does when confrontation is required, we can better prepare to take appropriate action.

As a police officer, I've encountered literally thousands of people that I would consider confrontational to some degree. Some have been to the far left and are upset at their situation, so they are verbally aggressive towards the arriving officers. We are trained to deescalate these verbal situations by remaining calm ourselves, talking slower, and using words that are not inflammatory to the agitated person.

Ninety percent of the time this technique works, and we can slow the person down enough to allow them to be far more communicative to us and allow us to better understand the problem and as such, hopefully resolve it for them. When you think about how often police officers do this every day, it is frankly dozens and dozens of times. After just a short time on the street, you will have been confronted and deescalated hundreds of aggressive people. Lesson learned, experienced gained.

Now to the far right in the life of a police officer, are those situations where upon arriving to a scene, an officer is confronted with physical violence.

Just as in dealing with an aggressive verbal attack, deescalating a violent physical attack requires equally as important immediate action by the officer. Unlike the verbal attack however, law and legal precedent far more come into play as to the actions allowed to confront them. If you are thinking we are wading back into the first "A" of our three principles, authority, you are correct.

Remember part of the authority I initially told you that I have been granted by Congress is the authority to defend myself and to make probable cause arrests.

The officer must quickly already know and understand what authority he or she has that gives them the ability to take action. This is not too far removed from a supervisor confronted with a problematic employee. You must already know and fully understand what authority you have been given, so you can quickly take action to address your supervision problem.

Much like the far left and far right of the spectrum a police officer must know, only hopefully without the threat of death, as the officer may face.

Taking action as a leader is kind of the meat and potatoes of any leadership position. Knowing when to take action is the first part and taking some form of action is the second. The first, we learn with experience, with training and with mentorship. Often this first piece is a little more forgiving in timeliness and application.

Often as we learn if any one situation requires us to do something, we have the opportunity take a deep breath, remind ourselves of past experiences or lessons and then act. The actual action will depend more on your ability to control and overcome your inherent autonomic and sympathetic nervous system.

So how do police officers really control their responses to confrontational situations? Remember even they are human and have the same human response that even the most-timid, librarian-like young new supervisor on the shoe room floor. The easy answer is practice.

As I said, I've been confronted by thousands of people from the far left to the far right and every one of them was built upon the other and become my experience that I have used in every leadership position I've been in. You see, dealing with a murder suspect or a teenager caught shoplifting is all handled in the same way you have a conversation with an employee who has come in late for work once again. Calmly, with purpose and with authority.

You see when you really understand the authority you are acting under, it empowers you to feel confident that what you are doing is true and proper. It's the same way in a leadership position. First know what your authority is, and the action that must follow will come easier and will help you overcome the hormones that will be unleashed at the first sign of stress.

During my time on street, I had the opportunity to be a Field Training Officer or an FTO. An FTO is a coach to new police officers that have just come from the police academy. New officers are eager and ready to hit the street and put into play everything they learned in the previous months at the academy. This time in a police officer's life is much like the basic leadership course I wrote about while in the Navy. It gives you an understanding of many things in your professional career and prepares you at the most basic of levels.

Now it's not a course on supervision or leadership, but it is a course on law, authority, tactics and a hundred other things police officers may encounter. What it doesn't provide is experience. That's where the FTO comes into play.

As a new officer you are assigned three or four FTOs before you are ever allowed to independently operate as a police officer.

These FTO's walk you through hundreds and hundreds of requirements that the new officer must accomplish in their time with each FTO. This is where you gain experience and the day to day grind of law enforcement. Some make it through this time, others do not.

On one late night shift, I had a rookie officer that was about midway through his training program. He had a little bit of time and experience with a previous FTO but was still far from ready to be on his own. I had been with him for about two weeks at this point and he was now driving the police car while I was a passenger. As an FTO this transition from the new officer riding and watching to one of being allowed to have far more control is always difficult. This is a critical juncture in the training of new officers. If they are going to fail, often this is the time. Stress levels are as high as they have ever encountered and learning to multitask in ways, they have never believed possible all happen at once. Add in late night shifts, no sleep, remembering what they were taught in the classroom and now on the street...all comes to a head when they move over to the driver's seat.

On this night, we had just left the jail where he booked a suspect in on an outstanding warrant. A good arrest, low stress, yet requiring a certain amount of legal paperwork. He did a good job.

Just before we pulled into the police station ready to go off shift, we both noticed a car that was driving erratically. He called for a graveyard shift car to back us up and initiated a traffic stop because of safety to the public.

Again, albeit we were ready to go home for the night, it was a proper decision by a new officer. Just as we pulled the car over and began to walk up to it to make contact with the driver, I noticed the passenger and driver switching places in the front seat.

Now this is something that happens from time to time and it is always amazing to me to think that people believe the police officer looking in the back window and watching the vehicle mirrors, wouldn't see this happen. But they still try from time to time.

I waited to see if this new officer would notice the action taking place inside of the car and then see what he would do. I thought this was a great teaching moment. If he failed to see the movements taking place that would be very problematic from both an officer safety stand point and a legal perspective. When it comes time to potentially issuing a moving violation or a ticket, it's important to issue it to the actual driver of the car. You never want to be that officer in court who gets a citation thrown out because you issued it to a person that wasn't driving. Besides, going back to that that authority thing, it's illegal to falsely issue a citation or arrest someone without probable cause to believe they did or were believed to have committed the violation. Enough legal talk.

My young officer did in fact see the two occupants doing the ole switch'er roo up front. He yelled at me "they are switching drivers!" again, good work for this new officer. He was communicating with me, his partner. Just as he yelled, the car began to squeal its tires and tear off down the road.

As we both turned to run back to the police car, I was really hoping I'd see our graveyard shift patrol car showing up and take over at his point. Getting into a pursuit an hour after you were supposed to be home was not high on my desire list at that point. But there was no other car to be seen, so the pursuit belonged to us.

Now mind you, at this point in my career I've been in many vehicle pursuits.

I know from these experiences that you must take immediate action in a manner that is counter-productive to those silly hormones that are beginning to be unleashed in your system. Remember all that hypothalamus stuff from earlier?

When the chase is on, trust me, your body goes into full fight or flight mode! If you are not careful, depending on how intense the situation, it can cause you far more harm than good. Your heart rate is going off the scale, adrenaline is pumping fast and furious through your veins. You become very focused and even can get tunnel vision if you are not aware of what is happening and take control of your body.

Now, with experience you overcome that normally. I had plenty of experience and was acting very calmly and without emotion. My young officer on the other hand was about to explode. As I arrived at the passenger car door, I knew this would be his very first vehicle pursuit and again, thought about the teaching moment. I didn't realize just how much a teaching moment it would turn out to be. Now here I am 20 years later still telling this story. I'd say it was a lesson well learned.

This young officer jumped into the driver's seat and immediately hit the automatic locks on all the car doors.

This is one of those things that I had been teaching him to do when he gets out of the car on certain calls, but never had we discussed vehicle pursuits up to this point. His brain was in full lock down, just like the car doors. At first, I wasn't too worried as I tried multiple times at opening the car door, all while yelling at him to breath and unlock the car! What happened next, I knew it was going to be a long remainder of the night. I then heard the high-powered engine of this police car begin to continuously rev up RPMs until I thought the engine just might explode.

As calmly as I could, I look in the side passenger window and saw this young officer in full mental lock down. His eyes were fixed straight ahead at the car now roaring off into the night.

His hand was on the automatic gear shift on the column and he had not yet realized he had not put the car in gear. You can picture looking out your living room window in the middle of the night to see one police officer standing at the passenger side window yelling at "someone" in the driver seat to OPEN THE DOOR! All while the vehicle engine is a top-revolutions; red and blue lights on from the initial traffic stop and now, the siren has been activated.

After about a full minute of me increasingly raising my voice, now banging on the side window with my baton, I finally was able to break this young man's concentration to look over at me and realize he had locked me out of the car. Now, with the engine still at top revolutions, the siren still screaming in this otherwise quiet neighborhood, I was able to take my seat next to him. By now, I had lost my composure and was trying to scream over the wail of the siren. Just as I was trying to get him to take his foot off the gas before this powerful engine blew up; he figured out that he was not in gear and dropped the gear shift into drive.

Now if you have seen on television or maybe even in person what a drag racer looks like as it takes off from its starting gate; this was us on this fateful night in suburban America. That police cruiser surged forward so quickly we both felt our necks snap backward as the rear tires engaged and we began to spin and smoke and burn so much rubber you would have thought the entire street was on fire. The sound was incredible, the smell was horrible and the car in front of us? Nowhere to be seen.

We quickly caught up to the fleeing vehicle with front seat jumpers and the pursuit was on. Through neighborhoods, back into town and the central business district, back through some neighborhoods and around we go. It was comforting to watch other police cars finally begin to join us in this "learning event" that I had earlier thought this simple traffic stop would have turned out to be.

As I slowly was able to get my young officer to shift his focus to also listen to me as I provided him direction on how to calm down, breath, start looking at all his surroundings and not be so locked in on the car a head of us. Remember as police officers we are responsible for whatever happens in these situations. Anyone hurt on the sidewalk, any car crashes that may occur, damages and so on all fall to the city for responsibility.

Just as I was feeling like I had control of my officer and he was calming down a bit, I watched to the amazement of my eyes, as the car in front of had driven full speed through the drive-up teller lane at a local bank. Now you have seen how wide those lanes are right? As we approached the same drive up teller lane I noticed we had slowed to about 60 mph! I screamed for him to stop the pursuit! Stop the pursuit! Stop the pursuit!

Knowing that there was no way we were going to make it through that teller lane at that speed. As we continued to approach, I realized he did not hear me once again and all I could do was close my eyes and wait for the impact. Woooosh! That police car flew right between the two posts of the bank and the next lane ATM machine without touching a thing… I was shocked to still be alive!

Now as I continued my less than calming screams at this young officer to slow down, pull over and terminate this pursuit, he was once again locked onto the car ahead of us.

For the next 15 minutes we continued through the city, through more neighborhoods, and finally ended up on what I knew was a road that had only one way out. I was feeling good that this was coming to an end as the car came to the dead-end of the road. It was then I watched the fleeing car drive right through dead-end marker and into a very large fruit tree orchard. The next thing I remember was we were once again threading the needle, this time between two rows of trees. I remember watching those tree trunks barely missing each side view mirror.

Then as quickly as it began, it came to an end as both cars slowly began to decrease speed and sink into what can only be described as 18 inches of saturated, gooey, slimmy mud!

This story ends with my young officer on foot pursuit and eventually catching both occupants knee deep in mud, then walking them back to the police car. I was already trying to explain to the shift Sergeant why we had been so reckless and now have a $40,000 patrol car stuck in the middle of an orchard. I must admit, it did help that the rookie officer caught the two individuals, but only a little.

So why is this story about a police officer learning some hard lessons early in his career so important in this book about leadership principles such as; **Authority=Action=Accountability?**

I believe it touches all three principles rolled up into one event, however here where we talk about taking action with the authority you have been given is really highlighted.

It's probably not too far fetched for anyone to understand that a police officer has the authority to pursue a vehicle and people involved in a crime. That's what cops do right? Chase bad guys; catch bad guys.

What I believe is important to know and understand here is the conversion of that young officers thought process to move from knowing, understand and having real authority to do something, onto taking real action based solely on that authority. Why do police officers act so quickly in situations like this in taking action? How might that help you as you lead a young group of shoe salesmen on the department store floor?

Police officers act quickly and often take swift, immediate action to situations unfolding before them for a variety of reasons. One being safety of themselves and the people around them, the citizens, home owners, pedestrians, other drivers and so on. Delaying action can honestly turn very dangerous for all those people, most immediately however is the officer.

Secondly, any delay in taking action by the officer sends a signal to the citizen, even if only a fleeting thought, that the action they just were a part of is, maybe isn't as bad or illegal as they first thought. I mean if the officer doesn't really care or doesn't act, then it must not be that bad.Think about how often you drive over the speed limit every day.

We all do it, because we know that the action of officers is limited to stop us in most cases. We know speeding is often not high on the priority list of problems the police must deal with every day and as a result we begin to tell ourselves that speeding a little bit is ok.

Not so far off from an employee whom you fail to address quickly a small problem in the shoe department with an employee. If you don't immediately address even the smallest of issues, it becomes "ok" in the eyes of the employee.Soon minor speeding becomes major speeding.If you are never stopped by the police or put in check in how your speed problem continues to evolve and grow, then your take on traffic laws becomes more distorted as time goes on. Of course, when you see others being stopped; when you see red and blue lights on the side of the roadway what is the first thing you do? Slow down right? Of course, so goes life as an employee. When leaders take action on poor performers and the rest of the office sees the red and blue lights, they correct their actions, even if for only a short time.

If you're a supervisor and you know you have the authority to handle a problem with one of your employees, like this young officer knew, the important next step is; take the action. What if that young officer had not done anything that night when he saw the two people jumping over each other in the front seat to disguise the real driver? I don't know about you, but I want the police officers in my community taking immediate action when they see an issue unfolding before them.

I don't want them afraid to act or scared to act or unable to act, I want them to act and act now.So goes the young supervisor in any organization. I want my newest supervisor to understand what authority she has and when an issue comes up, to act. That's what I hired her for.

As for that young police officer who learned many lessons that night about having authority and taking immediate and decisive action. He later in his career would be faced with having to react to a suspect pulling a gun on he and his partner. He knew his authority, he knew he had to take action and he did so, saving the life of himself and his partner. That's when I know small lessons learned early in anyone's career can pay off exponentially later in life.

"Action is the means by which everything is accomplished" -*Matthew Brandt*

CHAPTER 4

ACCOUNTABILITY

F inally, we add in Accountability to the right angle of our triangle. Accountability today seems to be the buzz word of leadership trainings as well as the media around the world. "Hold them accountable!" seems to echo the hallways of every board room and corporate office anywhere around the globe. The media is quick to dig its claws into anyone in a leadership position that is exposed in some way to having failed to monitor or act on anything at any level within their organization.

I'm the first one to lay blame on the Captain of the ship when he or she has direct knowledge and failed to act on any issue within their realm to oversee. The reality is however that the Captain of any ship, and I say this metaphorically for any business, has several layers of managers and supervisors below them that have been tasked to carry out actionable items to ensure the machine stays well-oiled and running smoothly.

The Captain relies on those layers of oversight to lead, guide and manage the workforce. When that doesn't happen and when the Captain knows the issues are there and still fails to act, then I'm with the media, it's time for the Captain to go. That's a failure of leadership at the highest level. If this is an issue you have today, save some time and skip to the chapter titled "You Suck It's Time To Go."

I spent about five years aboard the USS Duluth LPD-6 stationed out of San Diego, California. This ship was about 600 feet long and carried around 380 crew and an additional 900+ U.S. Marines when they were embarked. On this morning, we had been out to sea, off the coast of California for just a couple days of training with the local Seal Team cadre there off the beach near Coronado. Pretty mundane stuff for most of the ship's company. We all went about our business of running the ship and all its very busy pieces.

My job and that of my division was to care for all the weapons systems on the ship, including small arms and about 28 train car loads of ammunition we stored for those embarked Marines. It was a normal busy morning, we were up early as we knew we were headed back into port that morning.

As San Diego was our home port, the entire crew had been in and out of this port many times and the transit of the ship canal down to 32nd St. Naval Station was routine. Navigators knew the course to take. The deck crew that handled things like the steering of the ship, the anchor system and all the look-outs watching from every vantage point on the ship. The engineering crew knew their job in ensuring the rudder was working well, and the engines could be counted when needed.

What could not be counted on as routine that morning were the officers on the bridge that morning, our leaders that had control of that huge ship coming into port. We came in early, around 7:AM or 0700 in Navy time. That was not unusual, ships came and went early from the port and it meant early liberty (or time off) for the crew that day. What was different than most port entries this morning was how very foggy it was. Most of the crew noticed the fog and thought it a bit unusual to try to make the large arching curve of the San Diego channel in the fog. Again, doable with all the electronic radars available and how many times Duluth had made this transit without any problems. So, in we headed anyway.

About 20 minutes into our transit required our turn to starboard, a right hand turn to remain in the center of the channel and well within the depth needed under her keel. The navigators were tracking exactly where the ship was by the minute.

They had excellent radar points to triangulate, they had visual confirmation from lookouts on both side of the ship and they were relaying these points to the Officer of the Deck. The OOD is the person who at any given time has control of the ship. He or she is in charge and responsible for the actions of everyone on the ship at any given time.

Now of course the Captain is always ultimately responsible for the ship and its crew, but Naval protocol for ships at sea is that when you are qualified as the OOD at sea, you have all the knowledge and experience to drive that ship. This morning, the Captain was on the bridge but by protocol the OOD was in charge. There was also a Junior OOD assigned which is just a junior officer that is learning how to become a fully qualified OOD.

All very normal for any Navy ship underway. On this day, the JOOD had been making the navigational corrections to this point and had been answering the Navigators recommendations. The Navigator and the JOOD for the most part had been the two "driving" the ship that day. Again, not all that unusual as JOODs must learn at some point how to drive ships in critical times.

The Navigator advised the JOOD and OOD that he recommended "a turn to starboard" was required in 300 yards. Neither the JOOD or OOD responded by repeating back the recommendation of the Navigator. It should be noted here, that one of the jobs of a junior enlisted Sailor that works on the bridge is the keeping of the Ships Log. It is literally where every action, every course change, every order of the OOD, the engine room, everything that happens on that bridge is written down in this log. That young Sailor is trained to do nothing else, while he or she is on duty but to listen and record for prosperity everything that is said, in the order it is said.

It has been Navy policy and tradition since the days of John Paul Jones and the six original Frigates of the U.S. Navy. On this day, the actions of that Sailor would prove to be like a court reporter listening to a witness lay out what happened at the scene of a crime. He did a fantastic job in recording everything that took place before, during and after this quickly unfolding problem.

The Navigator then recommended a "turn to starboard in 100 yards", again no reply from the JOOD or the OOD. The Navigator recommended (with a little more urgency) an "immediate 30 degree turn to starboard to remain in the channel." Still no response from the JOOD or OOD. Now during all this time, the Captain had been on the bridge wing, which is just outside of the interior of the bridge itself and on the other side of a closed door, so he could not hear what was being said and what was unfolding on the bridge. The look-outs that were stationed at all four corners of the ship were now reporting the ship was approaching multiple small sail boats at anchor.

Remember now, nobody had said anything to the engine room, so they believe the requested speed of the ship was exactly what was needed and continued to ensure the ship stayed at speed.

Now what unfolded next happened in less than 30 seconds and with it the careers of three men ended. One the Captain, one the senior OOD and third the JOOD that had recently graduated from the United States Naval Academy with a bright future ahead of him.

The Navigator was now yelling at the OOD that he recommended "an immediate and emergency hard starboard rudder to avoid collision!" At the same time, it was then that all forward look-outs could be heard and seen, pointing; "multiple small craft directly under the bow!"

The Combat Information Center or CIC (those watching the radars) could also be heard over the radio now screaming about the pending collision with multiple small crafts. The Captain then could hear the screams on the bridge and ran inside to try and take account of what was happening. He immediately yelled "Captain has the con!" which in as quick a way as he could, meant he has relieved the OOD and taken over all the duties of the OOD and in this case, the JOOD (the Captain can do that at any time, because he's the Captain and it's his ship.)

The Captain then yelled "All engines back full!" signaling the engine room to reverse the engines at maximum speed. As if this wasn't enough, those on the bow of the ship that were charged with handling the anchor could see that the mighty war ship was driving directly into a sail boat marina just off the edge of the channel on the north side.

Anchored there were maybe a hundred or so 20 to 50-foot sail boats of all shapes and sizes. The Chief on the bow, requested permission to "immediately drop the port anchor" to help slow the ship and minimize damage. His request was also not repeated and not acknowledge by anyone on the bridge. In all the confusion during the time the Captain had assumed control (mere seconds earlier) and the Chief's request, neither the Captain or anyone on the bridge had thought to respond.

The salty old Chief on the bow who had more time at sea than anyone on the bridge driving, did what he knew he needed to do. He ordered the port anchor released. That 22,500lbs anchor fell at incredible speed and with a remarkable rumble and with a horrific crash into the water. The ship was now doing is best to stop forward motion and reverse power under two giant engines and propellers, all at the same time that anchor fell directly next to a 40-foot sailboat, nearly crushing it to pieces.

At this point the 600-foot ship, with hundreds of crew members onboard were coming to a screeching halt as best a ship on the water can. I remember the feeling of that giant ship rocking and moving, the engines at full speed in reverse, the shaking, the noise and just knowing that something had gone terribly wrong that morning on this routine trip back into port.

As the ship came to a very abrupt halt. The anchor and its very large chain took hold in the muddy bottom of the channel. The engines were still whining at full reverse until the order of "all stop!" by the Captain. Everyone was now silent; we looked at each other in disbelief of what had just happened.

What had just happened was a massive break down in leadership. It was a key moment in my life from my own leadership perspective. I had already been supervising and leading more and more junior Sailors and was no longer trying to learn the basics of supervision. I was learning to apply higher levels management theory and was working on the development of my three A's of leadership. I had already spent nearly three years in the Reagan White House and had absorbed, learned and evolved from a 19-year old kid to that of a young man that was learning quickly what both good and poor leadership looked like. On this day, on this ship, it was like looking through an x-ray in a doctor's office; I could see inside the problem while it was right before my eyes.

Shortly after the ship had come to a stop, it was noticed that there was a man in the water, just off the port bow. The ship immediately went into emergency man-overboard procedures and launched a rescue effort. It turned out the man in the water was the owner of that small sail boat we had just nearly destroyed.

We later learned that he had been awaken in the early morning by a weird feeling and uncommon calmness on his sailboat. He peeked outside to see this massive 17,000-ton ship looming in over the top of his now ever shrinking sail boat under the massive showdown of Duluth. He knew the collision was imminent and jumped into the San Diego harbor just moments before that anchor was released and shook his sail boat like a typhoon.

After his rescue that morning, we all watched in dismay as the ship went to "flight quarters, flight quarters, flight quarters!" this was how we prepared for accepting inbound aircraft or prepared to launch helicopters from our flight deck. We had a large flight deck that although not for fixed wing airplanes, could land and launch pretty much any size of helicopter. The next thing I remember was watching a large Navy helicopter inbound and then land from North Island Naval Air Station which was just across the channel to our south.

I could see from my vantage point, the Captain, the OOD and the JOOD all headed to get on the helicopter. They had an armful of navigation charts under their arms and that "ships log" that had recorded everything that morning. We never saw any of those men again onboard Duluth. All three had been relieved of duty.

What really went wrong that morning and how do we learn the lessons from it. Let's look deeper first at accountability and how the Navy goes about changing future behavior. Then where do all of the three A's are fall into play in this extreme example of failure. You must remember that the Navy has been building, sailing and fighting at sea for more than 200 years.

It is well known for its long history and traditions that honestly have not really changed so much since the days of wood ships and taking on pirates off the coast of Tripoli. What the Navy did then, in many ways remains what the Navy does today in how it manages and protects its ships.

What many may not realize is that a U.S. Navy Captain at sea, meaning the ship is not alongside any peer or under anyone else control, that person has as much authority as any single person in the United States. I'm talking from the President, a federal judge, clergy, law enforcement, you name it and is only bound by the law of the sea and the U.S. Constitution. A Captain at sea has enormous powers that truly nobody else in our country has, and it's given to him or her by law.

The Navy uses that enormous power to look at accountability just a little bit different than I do in the three "As." Outside of this single position of a Captain at sea, in charge of vessel at sea, maybe only a pilot of an airplane will you find accountability mean something other than changing behavior. If the Navy saw accountability to mean the need to change behavior, it would on many occasions take events like this as a learning opportunity.

They would try to retrain, educate and use, the 30 years of experience at sea that in this example this Captain had and continue to get more use of his experience and skill set. However that is not the case.

The Navy gives that enormous power to a Captain at sea with the understanding that he or she is 100% responsible for every person, every action, every success and every failure, without waiver. The Navy changes behavior of future Captains by holding current ship's Captains accountable through zero failure options.

Instead of retooling, retraining, re-educating and reusing all that experience of a Captain, when one fails in any way, they fire him and move on to the next one.

It's an antiquated means of changing the future behavior of people, and in my eyes the senseless waste of unequivocal experience that is lost forever.

The Navy counts on the fact that for every Captain at sea there are 100 people equally experienced, capable and ready to assume that command. What I have seen in some areas of corporate culture are similar manners of leadership and structure. It is also the same thought process that today's media and our social networks seem to use when there is some failure at any level. Any part of human error requires the immediate termination of the highest-ranking person.

Considering all the recent issues our Navy has had in the past decade with ship collisions and loss of life (there have been multiple) I often wonder will the Navy ever decide to break the age-old tradition of holding the Captain accountable for the mistakes of every person below him? In this case, a mid-career Navy Lieutenant with solid experience and training and a brand-new graduate of the Naval Academy saw their careers end. What a waste of talent and resources in my opinion.

Was there a lapse in communication that fateful morning? Absolutely! Could there have been better oversight by the Captain?

Of course! Did the OOD put too much pressure on the very young and inexperienced JOOD, that eventually saw him lock up and fail to act at the most critical of times? Again, yes! Could all their failures in accountability have caused the potential for unknown millions of dollars in damages and even the deaths of individuals? You bet it could have.

Was this a massive lesson learned for the Navy, for everyone else on that bridge and for that Chief on the bow that gave the order to "let go the anchor!" indeed it was life changing for everyone.

We all took the lessons from that day into the rest of our careers and went on to lead many, many others in all walks of the Navy and later across the business world.

Makes you think a little more about accountability and if we use it effectively today. My belief was then and remains today that accountability it is truly meant to change behavior and not punish.

What I believe is very important to you right now as you read along and try to glean key elements from the three principles of leadership (Authority=Action=Accountability) is to understand that accountability is never, and has never, been about punishing anyone. It's never been about terminating employees or leaders at any level based on failure to take action. Unless…their failure to take action has been allowed to continue unchecked and has now moved into criminal behavior. That's an entirely different conversation. Once that transition from human failure to criminal behavior has taken place, then there is but one way to move forward and that is termination.

In my opinion however, those are few and far between. Except for the work of the main stream media and our social media platforms, instant videos and such that all go directly for the throat of the Captain.

Accountability is simply about changing behavior. The reason we link accountability to the cut-throat tactics of politics and high-level c-suite leadership falls both fully in the lap of the media and our antiquated early supervisory training, or lack of it.

In the rest of the world, where hard work takes place on the sales room floor, on the factory line, in the cities and companies around the world, accountability means something entirely different.

At the end of the day, being accountable for your actions (doing the job you were hired to do) is all that matters. If you are doing that and doing it in a way that does not cause friction or tension with your coworkers, then you are probably doing what is expected.

Going above expectations is great, but that's not the purpose of our conversation here. Meeting expectations is where accountability comes into play.

Who is accountable to whom? An employee is accountable to his or her supervisor and the company or organization. Show up on time, dress appropriately, learn your job, do your job and in return the employee expects to the organization to be accountable for paying them for those services provided. That's a job, that's what it's about. Someone provides work, effort, service to an organization in a way that organization has asked (again assuming legal and above board) and in turn the employee is compensated. So really, every employee is in the service industry even if your company isn't.

Are supervisors, managers and leaders accountable? Of course, they are; to their higher-level managers and maybe the board of directors or CEO, even to the employees below them. What about to the stakeholders or citizens they serve? What about to the suppliers of the raw material it takes to build the company's widgets. Yes, the too depend on the accountability factor. That means we are all in the service industry and we are all accountable? Yes! That's the point!

Secondly let's talk authority in this incident. Who had the authority to keep this collision from happening? Obviously, the Captain did, he was required to ensure anyone on his ship that he placed in control as Officer of the Deck was fully trained, experienced and capable of handling not only "routine" events, but significant emergencies. Remember this is a U.S. warship that had previously been and would again be in, a major battle conflicts at sea. Knowing how to handle a variety of critical incidents is required of the Captain and the OOD on duty.

Did the Junior Officer of the Deck have any authority here? No, actually he did not, his authority lay with the OOD, he was there to learn, so he thought.

Now I'm no longer in the Navy and I'm very proud of my time spent serving both at sea, at the White House and as a Drill Instructor at Navy basic training. I also know that I grew a great deal as a leader that day and most of the men standing beside me did so as well, in more ways than one. So how do we transfer this lesson learned into today's hectic world of global business?

I think other than pointing out the outdated accountability method that the Navy continues to use, there are several lessons here. First is communication between the many levels of management. Knowing whom was in charge at the time, who had the authority to make any decision that day, and then who did or did not take action?

Can you see this same lesson taking place in your organization today? It may not be about running a ship into sailboat marina and nearly crushing a boat with its anchor, but what about the policies in your company and how they impact your workforce? What do your first line supervisors do every single day to empower, teach, mentor your workforce?

What are you doing as the CEO to embrace a culture of empowerment, communication, inclusion, mentorship, and equality in your workforce?

Do you have the ability to have hard conversations with employees, especially your supervisory team over their performance?

So many questions can be asked and it all circles right back to what is your authority? What actions are you taking?

And are you creating a culture of accountability to ensure the behavior you want from your employees is being managed properly?

I said earlier in this chapter that accountability is about changing behavior. If you think about it in those terms it will help you better understand what you are wanting and trying to do when itcomes to dealing with employee issues. Stop listening to the media about "hold them accountable!" To them, they are looking to sell air time with the breaking news of someone being fired. Plain and simple. Do you really believe that CNN, ABC, FOX any of them really have you, the line level employee at heart when they break these news stories? No! of course they don't, they don't have a clue about nor do they care about the employees in any organization.

They use the term "accountable" because they have created this frenzy around the term and instigated a movement around accountability. I can almost picture the news teams standing behind the masses that have come together to "hold someone accountable" and they are smiling and smirking about the firestorm they created, all while taking notes and writing the breaking news story.

Again, it goes back to my initial thoughts about how the Navy treats its most senior leaders based on 200+ years of leadership.

Total authority = total accountability. The Navy doesn't do this at any other level of management or leadership. If a young Sailor is supervising a small group of Sailors and one of her subordinates make a critical mistake, they don't terminate that young supervisor's career. They retrain, they mentor, they help build her into a better leader so the next time something comes up, she is better equipped to handle the problem, any problem!

So why do we not want to change behavior of our managers and leaders when they fail in some way? Why go straight to termination? Again, aside from doing criminal stupid... That's a non-starter, and no one will disagree.

Unfortunately, that does happen and for those leaders at any level that lose sight of their character, their ethics, the core values in life and business, we sign them up for the "You Suck, It's Time To Go" chapter.

CHAPTER 5

LIES, HIDES AND FAKES

One question that I've been asked many times and one I've heard posed to many leaders is; are leaders made or are they born? Early on in my career I wondered the real answer to this question. I saw many leaders that in my opinion were so good, so well-polished in how they interacted and led that I was certain they had to have been born that way. You could feel it when they walked in the room. The command presence just oozed from their pores. People sat up a little straighter when they were around, and people just listened intently with what they had to say. This could not be learned I thought. You either have "it" or you don't. Many leaders didn't have that special characteristic that made people buy in and fall in line with that leader's vision.

People may not always like a leader or the vision they bring to an organization but when you're a good leader, I mean a really, good leader...people listen, and people want to follow you. There have been plenty of leaders that had "it" but used it in ways that was counterproductive to that of a great leader. Adolph Hitler convinced an entire nation that he was the one they should follow and if they did so, he would rebuild their nation. It worked until it until went too far as we all know. Bill Clinton was an extremely charismatic President and leader. He sucked the air out of room when he would enter it, people adored him. As we know he too used his charisma and charm for nefarious reasons.

Then there were the likes of President Ronald Reagan. If you hang around me very much, you'll know that I'm a huge fan of our 40th President and his leadership. Having spent some in the Reagan White House, I had a front row seat to several moments of leadership under his guise. President Reagan in my eyes absolutely had the "it" factor when it comes to leadership. When he walked in the room, the air was sucked out, in a good way.

The aura of the room would change. It just did. Sure, you can say, "well he was the President of the United States" of course he's a leader and certainly people will be different around him. It was more than that, a lot more.

One thing that President Reagan had going for him was his background and experience in the movie industry. He was used to being "on-stage" in front of other people. Frankly that is a huge part of being a leader. When you are comfortable speaking in front of others, the more confident you look and feel and as such, people tend to listen better.

Think about some of the leaders you've had or seen around you. Those that struggled at talking on camera or in front of the organization, seemed to struggle at being a good leader.

It didn't hurt that he was also a large man. In this case size does matter when you are the leader of the free world. Of course, size is not completely a game changer. There are plenty of good examples of shorter men and women being great leaders. But here we are talking about the perception of leadership and how some, grew into fantastic leaders equipped early on with some advantages built in. Not everyone has those attributes when they assume a powerful leadership position.

What about the leaders in your company? Maybe you're at the very start of your career and are watching your supervisor lead. You watch her every day as she makes some poor decisions. She talks a big talk and tells everyone around her that she holds her people accountable! Nobody gets anything past her! She's the boss! The reality is, and you watch it every day, that she fears her own leadership shadow. She rarely makes an independent decision, and she never addresses issues with your peers in the workforce. She's all talk and no action.

I call people like this part of the lies, hides and fakes crowd. Unfortunately, they are everywhere, at all levels of an organization and as you are aware, in both private companies as well as our own government. Politics is the leading cause of this syndrome. They are a bit like Sasquatch; everyone talks about them, a few people have seen them, and yet nothing every becomes of them.

I saw this similar chapter title on an article I read and thought to myself; self, how appropriate is this title in today's world of leadership. We are seeing such a vast array of up and coming leaders today and many are simply faking it until they hope to make it. But whose fault is that really?

What is your goal as a leader of your organization? Not the organization's goals or mission, but yours. The new supervisor or the new leader in the organization. What goal or goals do you have for yourself?

Most people will repeat all or some part of their organization's mission/vision statement about what it is the "company" does. You are telling me what your organization does or its mission to do… Not what you do or what you would like to do. What are YOUR priorities in the organization?

I can tell you as a plank owner of the second largest department in the U.S. government, I've been here since the inception and I've seen behind the wizard's curtain in D.C. Many organizations are filled with lies, hides and fakes. Do you understand what I mean when I say "lies, hides and fakes?"

It's people that are managers instead of leaders. It's senior leaders, directors, executives and such, that may have been fantastic journey level employees, but were never taught how to become a leader in its purest sense. So, they play the "lies, hides and fakes" manner of leadership.

They are often the easiest to spot too. They are the ones with the largest egos, the greatest entitlement syndrome and the people that must control everything in their organization. Why? Because if it ever got out that their team, or their division or agency that they lead is failing in any way, he or she can quickly cover up the problem or redirect it in a way that makes it appear to be far less a problem than it truly is.

The first one; lies. Many people get proficient at lying about what they have done in the past, what they are doing, or what they plan to do next. They are perpetually coming up with great ideas, but never finishing them. Coming up with new concepts, having a vision of what the future looks like is not what I'm talking about. Those are traits of truly good visionary leaders. But the flavor of the month, with zero follow through as to what was accomplished, that's what I'm referring to. Do you know anyone like that?

Secondly; hides. Oh, we all know this person. He never seems to be around when the bill comes due to be paid. He never seems to be in the office to sign the end of year financial close-out. Never seems to be able to attend a decision meeting or whatever requires critical decisions at the most crucial time. Always, hiding when things get tough. Maybe this is the leader that says they were "mentoring" another leader, so he wants to give them the opportunity to take on the project. Or they are never seen by employees on the front line, working. They manage by email and phone calls. Stays behind their desk, afraid to engage employees face-to-face. They have forgotten where they started and the longer it is, the farther from their employees he falls.

Finally, the fake; Unfortunately, I think many organizations have far too many of these folks. I believe many leadership programs today have allowed this to happen.

Being a fake means you are faking any understanding of the organization, the problems at hand by the frontline employees, the job duties, the mission requirement, or what it really means to do the job of your frontline employee. They just truly don't ever understand what you are there to do. Often, these are the results of hiring a senior leader from outside the organization. They just don't ever learn your culture and company value.

I say the leadership training programs themselves have some culpability in this because qualified leaders, good people, often go through some of well-known senior training programs and become certified leaders. However, once they get anointed with the magic fairy dust as a certified executive, it's believed they should be able to lead in any field, in any organization. Really? Who ever thought that was a good idea?

Now don't get me wrong, well rounded leaders are better able to serve in most cases, but they should serve in the positions they are most qualified for. Serve in those careers they have spent a lifetime learning to do. Now remember I'm just talking about our leadership programs here. I do think there are some organizations where some slight differences but many similarities. When the CEO of Best Buy takes the job as CEO of Target or the COO of General Motors becomes the COO of...you name it. Those large corporations are about producing or procuring their widget(s) and selling them to a market. It's about organizational norms, it's about the stock holders, boards of director and company profit. Much easier cross-walk of skill sets. Not all leadership positions all this cross-walk to happen and be successful.

Finite vs. Infinite

Now let's talk about the games. There are two types of games people play in the corporate world. Finite and Infinite.

A finite game is one that is made up of a finite number of people or players, a finite goal in mind, and a finite time to play or the end to the game. Football for example is finite game. There are finite number of players, playing for a finite amount of time, with a goal of having or scoring more points that their opponent. We don't get to the end of a football game and say; "oh let's play five more minutes, I'm sure we can catch up." No; when the game is over, the game is over. Everyone understands a finite game.

An infinite game on the other hand is a game played where there is no finite goal to win it, there is no finite number of players that come and go. Nor are they added and dropped as the game goes on and the only purpose to be in the game is to outlast, outlive and outdo everyone until everyone else drops out.

Say the Cold-War for example. This was an infinite game being played by several countries, in several places with no real clear winner to be declared. Some countries fell away, while others joined the game. Russia vs. Afghanistan, the Russians were there to "win" while the Afghans were there to survive. To outlast them and regain their country. The U.S. in Vietnam; we were there to "win" and the Vietnamese were there to survive in their homeland.

All well and good, just so you know there is a difference; because when two people or two companies that are finite players playing a finite game, they are fighting for or competing for a goal, for a win and the time is limited. If one company is looking to beat the other company in sales, in product manufacturing, in new ideas, new widgets. That is their focus.

When you have two finite players or companies playing in the game, who are trying to outlast the other, they type of game matters.

That is what happens in most operations today, they try to simply outlast their competition until they either file for bankruptcy or merge with another company simply to survive in the game. Look around, how many of those actions have you seen in the last ten years?

Microsoft for a long-time was interested in out "geeking" Apple in every category. The best cell-phone, the best music device. They were constantly looking for ways to be better than Apple, produce a better device. On the other hand, Apple was ONLY looking how they could best serve teachers and students with products to make their lives better. One company was looking to beat the other company (finite) and one company was looking to just be in the game and outlast the competition with superior ongoing products (infinite.)

Who still listens to a Zune? What is a Zune you ask? Well that should be proof enough that the Microsoft answer to the Apple iPod was a fantastic device when it came out, but it never improved, it never evolved, it played the finite game, the game was over, they won, for just a minute, but they were playing a competitor that was playing an infinite game. Two very different games.

We could make the same comparison with Blackberry and Apple iPhone. Who still has a Blackberry? Who used to have one? Again, Blackberry was playing a finite game and Apple continued to play an infinite game. They again outlasted and continued to improve until they ran the competition into the ground of irrelevancy. Once your product becomes irrelevant to the world, so does your company. As a leader, as soon as you become irrelevant to your organization so does your stock in the company.

As leaders today, in this organization, do you know what game you are even playing?

Are you playing a game to simply win over the competitor or are you playing an everlasting game just hoping to survive and outlast the opponent?

For many organizations it's probably more along the infinite game, as your mission though different and specific probably has one common goal. The infinite mode of play, as they say on a favorite TV reality show; Outwit, Outplay, Outlast our enemies (other companies.) Then it's the matter of our long-term survival, so many of us will fall away, others will join the game and it will go on for some time.

But as leaders it is imperative that we know what game we are in fact playing in our organization. Some of you may have come from organizations that have been part of a very powerful finite game being played in-order to "beat" someone else.

Let's say now that someone that is playing or is used to playing a finite game is suddenly up against someone playing an infinite game. One wants so badly just to win, while the other is holding on for the long haul, because the long haul means we just hope to outlast the opponent. Will the finite player every be able to win this game? No, probably not; not unless he or she changes the game in which they are playing in their head.

As we bring on supervisors into our work place; great technicians, or awesome police officers, whatever it is your organization does and we promote them to supervisor, what do we do with them? Monday, they come in and now instead of being one of the team members, they are now put in charge of the team. Responsible for the team. Learning to lead is very much like any skill set in the world. It can be learned, it must be learned, and it must be practiced, or it will die.

Think of your parenting skill-set for those that have children. Most everyone CAN be a parent, but not everyone will or should be a parent. Some lack the drive an initiative, the basic skills and have no desire to learn them, that is ok! Those that do, do and being a parent, like being a new supervisor takes a new skill-sets, new patience, new thought processes and new skills learned. As parents, we learn those skills from our own parents and grandparents normally. In the work place if we are learning them simply by watching those above us, much like our parent modeling, it is one way, but it simply may not be the best way to learn these skills.

We must invest in our newly promoted supervisors. As a newly promoted supervisors in your company, I would demand training at some level and in some capacity. You are being asked to do a different job on Monday than you had when you left on Friday. You are being asked to be responsible for real people now, not just the widget or the product or service the company is here to provide. Being responsible for real people, their successes and their failures is a whole new ball game. These skills need to be taught from the ground up. They must be renewed, continued, expanded upon and never left to stagnate. What worked a year ago, two years ago, even five years ago, isn't going to work today.

So first you must understand what are really doing inside your organization. Are you falling prey to the three biggies; lies, hides and fakes? Remember this is not a self-licking ice cream cone. Just because you believe you're the greatest leader since Abraham Lincoln, doesn't mean your perception is the truth.

If we took a poll of your subordinate employees right now, marched them in here and asked them if you're leading or are you one of the lies, hides or fakes categories, what would they say? Gut check I know. Think about it.

Secondly; are you playing a finite game like football? One that has a finite number of players, a finite definition of when someone has won, and someone has lost? Or are you playing in a game that has an undetermined number of players, with no real winning or losing in the general definition and the only purpose is to outplay, outwit, outlast everyone else? Either game might be ok to be in, but don't be a finite player in an infinite game…you will never win, and the game will eat you up!

As a leader, learning how to lead is a never-ending process. Were you born with leadership qualities? Maybe, but I'd say more likely than not as you grew up you had good role models along the way and learned from them, even if you didn't realize it. Maybe you have a little more charisma or panache than the next person and people seem to follow you because of that. That will work for a while but the luster on that shiny new car will wear off sooner than you think. If you haven't done anything about acquiring some real skill-sets, you will fall into the likes, hides and fakes category quickly because you won't know what you are doing.

As a company we must be able to identify our lies, hides and fakes. It's probably not as difficult as you might believe. Look around, I mean really look around your organization. There are people that work very hard every day and produce. From the frontline workforce to the top in your organization, you can normally pick out those that get the job done, sell more widgets, or produce more customers. Then there are those that don't.

Jack Welch said many years ago when he was running General Electric, that he prescribed to firing the bottom 10% of the company every year. Simply cutting away those lowest producers in the organization, every year. This put into action a perpetual need for employees and leaders to produce, to sell, to build, and to be the best in their circle. Or at least not in the bottom 10%.

Now I don't necessarily prescribe to this same thought process, but I will say there is some merit to it in theory. I don't like the idea of the cut-throat mentality this may produce amongst employees, but as the CEO I can see how this would be impactful to your bottom line. Cut the worst employees, save the money on salaries and benefits as well as failed production, and those above will work even harder.

What I do see in this theory however is it will quickly find the lies, hides and fakes in any organization. You simply can't lie, hide or fake your way through a career that holds your feet to the fire to produce. I wish I could say that was true in the federal government but let me tell you it is not. Our government, as good as it is, allows lies, hides and fakes to forever come and go in our workforce. It's not productive for the organizations we work for, but for those of us that do work hard, produce products, lead with integrity and continually learn to be better; it's easy to rise to the top.

Unfortunately, I've watched far too many people do just enough to "meet standards" and keep their jobs where there is really no incentive to do more, be more, or produce more. In fact, those that do, must do more, because those that don't or won't, can get by without repercussions. I've often wondered how that bottom 10% theory of Jack Welch would look if he ever had been elected President and could change our governmental workforce structure.

As a supervisor or a leader in your company you may not be able to fire the bottom 10% of your workforce but you do need to be able to identify them and use the authority you've been given to take appropriate action. Normally this group of employees will make themselves known to you regularly. They will be the very ones that struggle to make it in to work on time or will be the first to leave at the end of the day. They will be the employees that seem to always find some form of trouble with other employees, other managers and often use more sick leave than anyone else. That's because they belong to the lies, hides, and fakes crowd.

Now that we know and can probably easily pick out the employees that fall into this crowd, how about the supervisors or managers in your company? I was recently asked to work with a large city law enforcement organization that was struggling with an ethics issue in their senior leaders. I won't tell you what city, but I can tell you that their problems were not unusual to any company or organization, be it governmental or private. Once leaders begin to allow their core values and ethical bar begin to slip, it spreads like a disease.

In this agency; those very senior leaders just below the Chief of Police were beginning to get very tired of the magnitude of effort required to run a large city's police department. It is very hard work; it takes a lot of time, effort, energy and leadership skills to do it correctly. This small group of leaders more likely than not fell into the lies, hides and fakes group. They had undoubtably been promoted into their current positions without a great deal of merit.

It was well known throughout the agency that three of the four had been personal friends of the Chief, and as such, were selected over much more qualified senior leaders to fill those Deputy Chief positions. Once in place, there was little recourse anyone in the department could take, except to watch and live with their continued failed leadership decisions. At some point, because they had been part of the lies, hides and fakes club early on in their career, they never learned good leadership skills, senior level management tactics and were not exposed to mentorship along the way.

When opportunities for them to fall prey to ethical missteps presented itself, they were more than willing and happy to jump in with both feet. They really didn't even know any better and thought that since they had been protected from real consequences in the past, that nothing would become of it this time. Unfortunately for them, real investigations took place and real criminal indictments came along with them. They were in full organizational collapse because of poor decisions made in selecting, promoting and trusting leaders that were never capable of leading at that level.

The unfortunate part is the organization, its many sworn law enforcement officers and hundreds of staff and support personnel all suffered because of it. The officers in the ranks didn't trust any of their leaders. The citizens of the city had huge trust issues in their police department, its leadership and its Chief. Now what do they do? They will eventually work through a long an arduous process of removing leaders over time, and hopefully replacing them with qualified and trained leaders.

This is a just a good example of how anyone in the lies, hides and fake crowd can rise to the top of any organization. Look for and expose these people any time you can.

Learn to never be associated with this crowd and become the leader you want to be, through slow and steady training, and experience.There is no shortcut for those that have risen to the highest levels of leadership in any organization and now lead with integrity and core values.

"We must be able to identify our lies, hides and fakes" *-Matthew Brandt*

CHAPTER 6

THE FEAR OF OFFENDING SOMEONE

I thought this was an important piece of the equation to discuss here. Inevitably as a supervisor or leader in any organization you will have to have difficult conversations with one of your employees. Decisions you make, work schedules, disciplinary problems, something will come up that you need to address that will not always be popular. Remember as a leader, you left the world of being friends with everyone the day you accepted the position of first-line supervisor. Your job duties changed, and your responsibilities changed. You went from a line employee doing the work of the company to a supervisor or manager ensuring the employees in your charge, do the work of the organization. That is just the beginning of popular and unpopular decisions you'll make in your new role.

Offending other human beings is something we often just can't avoid. It's also something we try to avoid at all costs. It's a tricky part of our DNA make-up. The fear of offending someone however, is often a stronger personality trait than the need to be a successful leader of a team or organization. What I mean is; as leaders or supervisors of any kind in any profession across the board we know and learn and understand that we must motivate and reward good behavior. We see it all the time where employees are given awards for good work. Be it a performance bonus or an informal recognition of some kind. Even untrained supervisors know (usually) to praise good behavior. I say normally, but it certainly is not always true.

What happens in your organization when an employee is not a star performer? For any reason, be it personal issues going on in their life where they can't engage fully and do the work they were hired to do. Or, if it's purely performance and they don't have the requisite training or experience, you may not be able to give that to them, either way, they are failing at your organization's mission.

What do we do with those people? As I've already said, most supervisors, managers and leaders have never learned how to address issues of poor performance and when to call it quits and move on. We promote great technicians (meaning employees that are top performers) at whatever it is they do. A great salesman, a great mechanic, a great lawyer, a great budget analyst; you name the profession and there is a hierarchy of employees from the bottom to the top. How do you get to the top? You be the best at the bottom and middle of the organization.

Being a great salesmen or budget analyst or police officer or fireman is a skill set that is learned through academics, experience and time. Then one day we promote him or her to a supervisory position to reward them for their efforts in being a great technician. We have a ceremony, we up their salary, we give them greater authority maybe, certainly greater responsibility but we give them little help or training on how to be a leader. Now performance starts to drop, we wonder what happened to this great field technician, this awesome line level employee, salesmen of the year! Now the whole team is failing. Remember our shoe salesman example?

Let's talk about one aspect of why I believe most people, without some specific help, will most often fail as a new supervisor or leader of an organization.

People in a polite society are taught through years of experience watching parents, family members, teachers you name it; interact with each other in a specific way. We see what being nice looks like, we watch and observe politeness and compassion time and time again. As we get older, we are taught to say please and thank you, to observe personal spaces of people, to be respectful of privacy of others, and over time, this trait is engrained in who we are in society today.

It's not an American thing, it's not a European thing, it's not even an Asian thing.... every culture has it and every cultural has various levels of what nice and polite is to them in their respective societies.

Like anything, if it's practiced over and over, if it's observed from a very young age, it becomes who you are in life and how you act and interact in society. Think about how you first learned your native language. You didn't know you were learning the language, but you were exposed to it over and over from people around you. You were corrected, taught, and even every single person around you was doing it. After a few short years, you were too.

Now let's talk about being nice, polite or even how having compassion are very different things and how you become what you live and experience and why that may hurt you in being a successful leader if you don't learn to manage it or change that trait.

Many of our most valued society norms are things like empathy, modesty, patience, trustworthiness, kindness, integrity. They are instilled in us at a very early age and over years of practice, they become part of our human nature. But then you think about that childhood friend who is just the opposite.

He has little respect for others, their property or they are just known to be mean, with little remorse, or have any sense of societal manners in them. Of course, we also know many of these same folks end up involved with our criminal justice system as they have little sense of empathy, politeness, caring, or especially integrity. How did they end up different than you?

Politeness refers to the tendency to be respectful for others versus having aggressive tendencies.

It's about good manners and adhering to societal rules and norms. More than the laws of the land, but the expectations our society, from wherever in the world you are...every society has its set of norms. It's what we expect to see in upstanding, decent folks or "good people".

In contrast, compassion refers to our tendency to be emotionally concerned about others versus being cold-hearted. Much like we'd see in the proverbial "good Samaritan." They really worry about the well-being of others.

Some can see that politeness and compassion are two characteristics that go hand in hand, but they also separate from one another in very interesting ways. One study shows that politeness is associated with a conservative outlook and more traditional moral value, while compassion is associated with liberalism and progressive values.

Politeness and compassion are linked to different brain systems. Politeness with those governing aggression and compassion with those regulating social bonding and affiliation. In other words; politeness is a trait that helps our brain to keep us from being aggressive towards each other, or in any situation we are in. If you have a strong "politeness" trait, you will be less likely to be comfortable with confrontation or aggression. If you are a compassionate person you are far more likely to be a social butterfly type, someone that likes being around people, talking, bonding and creating relationships.

Your brain is structured from an early age to be both polite and compassionate but often one trait is stronger than the other, although most of us have at least a little of both in them.

To illustrate it a bit better, one study conducted what is called the "dictator game", a task in which a person is asked to divide a fixed sum of money with an anonymous stranger. The results showed that traditional economic predictions were wrong on all accounts. Not only did people NOT behave selfishly, they behaved in different ways depending on their personality.

Notably, polite people were more likely to split the money fairly than their rude counterparts.

Surprisingly, we did not see this for compassion, which may indicate that sharing money with a stranger won't necessarily arouse emotional concern. Here compassionate people gave away more money than their cold-hearted counterparts. Polite by-standers were not selfish per se, we know this because they were willing to part with their money just a bit quicker in this experiment.

But they were also more likely than anyone else to intervene when bearing witness to the mistreatment of others. This experiment highlights crucial differences between being good citizens and good Samaritans. Polite people don't necessarily help those in need, but they are fair-minded and peaceable. Meanwhile, compassionate people aren't necessarily even-handed and rule-abiding, but they are responsive to the misfortunes of others.

How does this translate into different kinds of behaviors and why is it important to know this as a leader or supervisor? Supervisors and or leaders must be able to deal with poor performance, disruptive behavior, negative work product and so on. We've all heard that supervisors spend 80% of their time dealing with 20% of their workforce. I believe this can easily be reversed to spending 80% of your time providing positive leadership to 80% of your workforce and relegate just 20% of time to the issues at hand.

There is no one specific trait or task that any leader can do that will be 100% effective. There are however a few things that will help your employees better understand your requirements and in the end; allow you to hold them accountable for their actions. Remember accountability is about changing behavior and not punishment. Look to ensure the behavior you want is easily laid out for anyone to easily understand and for labor attorneys to defend.

Provide specific expectations: Early in every employees career you must outline what exactly you expect from the employee in every aspect of his/her work. Work schedule, tasks, output, behavior, dress, communication. If you are a new supervisor to the group or a new leader in an organization, it's all scalable.... And it can be detailed at any point in the relationship and understand this is a relationship you are building. I suggest you do this upon your arrival to the team and then at least quarterly there-after to remind and re-instill your expectations. Many studies have shown that employees want and expect to be given these, so they know what it is the supervisor or leader wants them to do.It simply makes it easy on many levels as you engage and improve the workforce and when the time comes to remove someone from the workforce.

Get to know your team: One of the greatest mistakes new supervisors or organizational leaders make is not first getting to know their team. Even if you were a line employee and promoted into the supervisory position, you must take the time to know your entire team. Sit with them, have coffee, know their kid's names, their hobbies, what makes them tick, what problems are they facing and how they see themselves being most productive in this organization.

Provide regular and consistent feedback: This is true for a first line supervisor to line employees as much as it is for senior leaders pushing information to the organization on a regular and consistent basis. Employees want to know what is working, what is not, what it is they are doing matters. This may also be the first opportunity for you to know when someone, a team or parts of the organization are going off the rails in some way. As soon as you learn of an issue, provide that corrective action immediately. Document this feedback. Document any conversation, formal or informal. Documenting is not a novel on War and Peace, it's a simply paragraph with names, dates, times and basics of the conversation.

Authority=Action=Accountability:This is the heart of my leadership principles. The three A's are a simple yet an extremely effective tool to teach new supervisors as well as all employees and even senior leaders about empowerment and accountability. These three are separated by an equal sign because they all equally as important to each piece as they are to the whole process. Every person is given some degree of authority in the job tasks they are asked to do for the organization. What many fail at; is knowing exactly how much authority that really is. More authority in some minds means more work, so they want to diminish really all that they can and should be doing…. that's a problem. Action…is the work that you do, the widget you build, the sales you need to close, the accounts you need to grow…we can either take action or no action depending on the circumstances, but it must happen…action must take place to successful. Finally-accountability.

Accountability is not about punishment for bad behavior. It's about correcting or improving a behavior. However; failure to hold an employee, a team and organization accountable is the certain death of an organization.

It will rot it from the inside out. It will grow like a cancer amongst everyone who is a part of the team. Holding an employee accountable or more appropriately not holding an employee accountable is normally a top reason for employee dissatisfaction with a supervisor or leader.

Politeness vs. Compassion: How that impacts you as a leader, a supervisor, an employee makes the previous four tasks null in void if you are unable or unwilling to learn how properly approach hard topics with people you know and work with.As a polite society we are engrained from infancy to learn to be both polite and have compassion. That's what makes us a reasonable society to live in. Think about that; if we didn't teach our children that; think what our society would be. It's easy to know the answer to that…it's what we see every time a major crime is committed in our society. These are people that did not learn, were never given the opportunity to learn, chose to ignore or because of mental issues are unable to learn those traits. Unfortunately, those same traits often keep us from being good leaders too.

In my "Stop Being Offended" program I go deep into not only how and why we are predisposed to these behaviors of not being able or comfortable confronting other people, but I will give you some easy to use tools to take on troubled employees, failing personnel, and disruptive behavior in your work place.

We must get past letting a small number of problematic, unresponsive, uncorrectable employees guide and direct the work products and morale of the entire team or organization.

The great thing about being a 30-year police officer, having worked the street for many of those years; I've learned by exposure to pure evil; how to ignore and overcome bad people.

I didn't ask for nor want to learn this trait because I started out just like all of you as an infant in a loving, positive family where I learned respect, dignity, ethics and proper behavior. But this line of work will teach you how the other side lives. I've just learned to turn those traits into positive leadership tools for employees that just didn't learn the same things or the same way I did.

CHAPTER 7

YOU SUCK IT'S TIME TO GO!

O k, you've worked long and hard at learning what authority you have in your position as a leader in your company. You've asked questions, you've read policies and feel pretty good about the progress you've made at understanding just all the tools you have in dealing with your team. You've developed some checklists of contacts in your organization that can answer those questions that may come up from time to time. You have your labor attorneys on speed dial to make sure you don't step over the line when it's time to instill some progressive discipline.

Just as quickly, you've learned how important taking immediate action is when confronted with some form of leadership dilemma. An employee not living up to certain organizational policies maybe? Habitually late for work, dressing unprofessional, maybe simply not getting her work done as timely as you have laid out over and over. At some point in your supervisory career you will have to have a face-to-face conversation about your employee's performance.

Holding people accountable for their actions as we know is about changing behavior. It's not about discipline, it's not about terminating their employment. It's simply not. I've hopefully made this perfectly clear by now. When someone (remember the human factor here) makes a mistake, whomever is responsible or has oversight, should hold them accountable to change their behavior in some way. Going straight to termination, without extenuating circumstances robs you and them of so much. Experience, training, knowledge, insight, mentorship and so on.

This got me to thinking, maybe leaders or managers, CEO's, supervisors, you name it; maybe they don't know how to address and deal with people face-to-face. Termination is the easy the way out really. In some cases, it's the only way you can go, but in most cases it's not worth it.

The one thing the police officers do is deal with problem people. That's what we do every day of our career. Your bad day equals my every day. Whom better to help figure out the sticky point in any supervisor's career when confronting difficult people comes to fruition. I've outlined a short list of easy to follow steps to help you prepare for and handle your first or hundredth employee discussion to address performance issues.

First, take a deep breath and learn to control you breathing. Before, during and after any encounter that you believe may raise your blood pressure. Remember the earlier part about how your DNA is going to go into play when your mind believes it needs to either fight or flee? Well that is about to take place, and you can't really stop it from happening.

What you can do however, is to learn to better control how it impacts your response. Your body has gone through this before. Trust me, everyone has had the adrenaline dump and has felt the release of those hormones. Every time someone jumped out at you on Halloween, or maybe you had a close call in your car on the way to work and had to slam on your breaks to keep from hitting someone.

The only difference here is you know it's coming, you know your body will react, so you can learn to control it better.

Breathing is the first and most important part of this preparation. The newer you are at it, the more you need to prepare and practice. Deep breaths; in through your nose, slowly out through your mouth. Do this any time you are startled or surprised to the point of feeling the anxiety level rise. For this purpose, the few minutes before you speak with the employee, take ten deep breaths and try to get your body to relax. It's probably already on its way up on the stress meter, so you want to do your very best to get it back down to a level you are more able to function at full capacity.

Secondly, always have any discussion about performance, especially poor performance in your office. Bring your employee to your desk, your office, or at a place of your choosing, not theirs. This is a subtle way to begin to instill in them, that you are in charge and you are responsible for their performance. You don't want to over due or over think this piece, but you control not only the time but the place for this conversation. It will also help you in controlling your emotions and reactions. You're in charge!

Next, be very clear and to the point. Ask direct and very specific questions. "Why didn't you finish the four sales calls yesterday?" "Why didn't you finish the forecasting report on Friday like you said you would?" "Why were you late for work by more than 30 minutes, every day last week?" When you start the line of questions that you need answers to, or that you are trying to elicit a response for, it's ok to be at sitting at your desk, while they sit across from you. Insist they sit, never allow them to stand while you sit.

This is the time you will want to concentrate on your emotions and your breathing again. You will have to think about it and be purposeful at doing it. Take a breath. Try to relax your internal core muscles. Watch their reactions. Watch their body language, their eyes, and listen to exactly what they say. What they say may be important to remember, even jot some quotes down for later use.

Question answers you are given. When you ask specific questions of someone about what it is you're are trying to hold them accountable for, they will have an answer in most cases. Follow up with more direct clarifying questions. They most likely will be attempting to redirect your thought process away from them, onto something or someone else.

When you ask clarifying questions such as: "you say you made several sales calls last week? Tell me how many you made; 5, 10, 20 calls?" Nail them down on specifics or try to. If they are lying, they will most likely not be able to give you any specifics. "You said you were working hard on the sales report last week?" "Working hard in what way? What parts did you finish?" These types of questions put you in the power position again. Trust me when I say that a power play is being made by your employee.

You have called them on their performance and are trying to hold them accountable. If they have not been fully transparent, they will become defensive and try to sway your thought process. You need to be in control here. Back to controlling your breathing, controlling your actions and acting like the leader you are. You are in charge here!

This is the point where you will need to decide if this performance failure is one that requires some form of progressive discipline or if you will use this to help change behavior for future actions.

Assuming we are aiming to change future behavior, this is where you will make specific statements and give very definitive direction. "I expect 15 sales calls made each day." Or "You will finish all of sales reports before you leave for the day, each day." The requirements need to specific and measurable. Something you can track, something they can easily identify, measure and there is no miscommunication on details. And always write it down! Even if just for your notes so you don't forget as to what exactly you gave them for directions.

Deadlines, you must set a deadline. It must be achievable and reasonable. I say this because at some point in the future you may have to defend your actions to a merit system protection board (MSPB.)

Though not a criminal court, they will tend to allow the supervisor far more leverage to lead if you, that supervisor, show that your expectations are reasonable and achievable. If you have requirements of your employees that is so far off normal or not achievable by any human, they are the entity that will call you on it. That is when organizations often must bring out the big check books to settle with employees that have nothing on their mind close to doing the work, but only collecting the settlement. So be reasonable in your expectations. It must meet the level that in the minds of any reasonable person looking in at the situation from outside, your expectations could be met.

Our next step here is to have consequences for failures. If this is the first or maybe even the second time you've had this discussion, it's time to show your hand. It's time to lay out what the future looks like for them if they continue to not meet expectations. This is the accountability discussion that everyone struggles to have.

When it's time to have this conversation, I suggest you do what any good detective does when it's time to get that final confession out of a suspect. Get up from your chair and walk from behind your desk. Pull up a similar chair that they are sitting in, (normally a standard office desk chair.)You may have to even pre-stage these chairs if you need to. Pull the second chair up in front of or just off the side, but as close to in front of them as you can. Get a little closer than even you may feel comfortable doing. Again, this may take some practice on your part before you do it for the first time.

As a Detective Sergeant, this is how I was able to get suspects to tell me things they didn't really want to say out loud. When you move into someone's personal space, ever so slightly, the conversations become extremely personal.

I at times would even go as far as put my hand on their shoulder or their knee, just to give that physical reminder that I'm "right here!" Now, I don't ever suggest doing that to an employee, that is inappropriate in a work place. But sitting close to and having a personalized conversation about their work performance is always "reasonable."

Once you have taken your position next to them, and slightly in front of them, and pulled your chair up close, now it's time to talk consequences. Lean forward a bit, look them directly in the eye and be very clear. "Sam, if you continue to be unable to make at least 10 sales calls a week and turn in your completed sales reports by Friday evening of each week, it may result in some form of discipline or even your termination" Then the most important question to ask…."Do you understand me?"

Now, assuming Sam wants to keep his job and continue with your organization, he hopefully will say "yes." This is the time where learning, mentorship and true accountability has its best opportunity to be successful.

As a supervisor, a leader, motivator, it's a perfect time to stand up and go back to your desk chair (take that position of power again not the up close and personal one you just used. Now go into the coach and mentor role.

"Sam, I want to help you succeed here, this is what I'm going to do to help you."Explain to your employee that the entire sales team depends on his success, as does the company and you as his supervisor. When he succeeds, everyone succeeds. Talk through some ideas that may help him with things like time management, report writing, interpersonal communication (cold calls) or whatever issues you are having. Maybe it's arriving late for work.

Talk to him about how he might set an earlier alarm, or help him with getting his kids to school, maybe readjusting his schedule if that would help. Become an advocate for your employee and find a means to help him succeed. Show him how everyone depends on his success.

It's a bit of peer pressure, but it's true. You want him to succeed in the end. You want to change his behavior to the positive. You want to hold him accountable.

Some of these techniques are going to be a little uncomfortable at first. If you're a female supervisor and are talking to an aggressive male employee, you may feel a bit intimidated and have some well-deserved fear. It's ok if you have another senior leader in the room with you when you have these difficult conversations. They should be in the back of the room, sitting quietly and should be told to never interfere unless an issue of safety or actual physical confrontation should happen. This is YOUR employee and YOUR conversation to have.

I can tell you I have to have these conversations several times with armed police officers. It is very uncomfortable when you have a potentially volatile employee that is legally armed with a weapon, learning that you are holding them accountable for their actions. What I do in those circumstances is simply have that other senior leader sit next to the employee in front of my desk, within arms reach and able to react quickly if need be. I've never had that need, but it's worth mentioning.

When I say have another senior leader in the room, this must be someone that is there to be your witness and your protection both for your physical well being but potentially in a future MSPB or other such personnel hearing.

I also suggest that any time a male supervisor is having these discussions with a subordinate female employee, it's always wise to have another senior (hopefully female) leader in the room. But have someone there. It may not always be possible, and you should never fail to be a supervisor based on the unavailability of someone to be with you. You have been given the authority to take just such action when it's needed, so do that.

You Suck It's Time To Go...

Now the time comes when you have made several attempts to change an employee's behavior to meet your expectations, or that of the company.

You have tried mentoring, you've had conversations and set clear, precise and measurable expectations. Still this employee continues to fail, and you can no longer allow the poison they begin to spread to your remaining productive team. Understand that at some point, when employees do not meet expectations and performance is failing, they will quickly impact the rest of your team. If you don't step in and remove the poison, it will spread, quickly. A failing employee is one thing, a failing team reflects on your ability to lead.

First and foremost, never make this decision on your own. Go to your human resources department or division and get them involved early in the process. They should not be caught off guard and the first time they are hearing about this problem employee is when you are needing to terminate them. Allow your human resource team, the company labor attorneys and any employee and labor relations entity you have be part of your decision and action.

I always have our labor law attorneys review all my attempts to correct their behavior, the performance expectations I had laid out and the results of all my efforts.

They get every document, every written correspondence, email, you name it. They then have a good understanding of all that has taken place and can defend me, and our organization should this termination not go well. Sometimes they have even told me that we can't go forward with termination because there isn't enough documentation to support it. That's on me, lesson learned. It's a lesson I've learned over the years. Document everything from the beginning.

The attorneys or the human resources department will then actually write the termination letter. My job then becomes the delivery person. The organization becomes the one terminating them. It's not personal, it's the organization. That also is important because you want the organization to have to defend the action, not you.

I then take the same exact initial actions when it's time to tell them they must go. I have another senior leader in the room, observing. I bring the employee in and quickly get to the point. I have their termination letter on my desk, in a file folder so they can't see it. I don't allow them sit down, so I move the desk chairs from in from of my desk. This requires them to stand in front of me. I stand as they walk in so it's not as weird or uncomfortable as it would be for me to be sitting while they stand.

I get straight to it. "Susan, we've had many discussions about your performance over the last six months, and I was very clear with you about my expectations. I provided you some guidance and mentorship about correcting those behaviors. As of right now your employment here has ended." I then hand her the file with the letter in it.

It's ok at this point to be compassionate with your former employee. You can tell her that you wish things would have turned out differently and wish her good luck in the future.Do not however, allow an argument to begin or for her to initiate any conversation about how she can improve, or how bad she needs this job for her family. Simply say and point to your other leader in the room and tell her "Joe will take you to your desk and help you clean out and walk you to your car." This makes the next steps very clear to her.

She is not going to get a chance to be left alone for the next several hours while she poisons her now concerned and compassionate fellow employees that you need to keep on task and positive with your leadership. Those other employees will see that being accountable for your failures in this organization are noticed and swiftly taken care of. It will become a learning moment for those left behind. Use it!

I've in a funny way titled this chapter; You Suck It's Time To Go because I use that language in some of my keynote presentations and in my training program titled; Creating New Leaders. I never really say that to an employee I need to terminate, because well it will come back to bite me in court I'm sure.

And, I'm truly a compassionate person that knows anyone who loses their job based on a failure of performance is struggling to survive, to be productive in their adult life and has just lost not only a source of income but potentially, health insurance coverage for their family, retirement accounts, and so on. It's a big deal and I take my part of this time in their life to heart.

With that, I know my job is to produce the best team, division, agency that I have been given the privilege to supervisor or lead. I have made a commitment, like you, to use my given authority, take reasonable and appropriate action and hold my employees accountable. I also know that I'm there to lead. With being a leader, you must be a consummate mentor, trainer, teacher, and do so with all the characteristics and ethics you want to see in your own leaders.

Never allow your ego to be your guidepost nor your emotions to be the road well walked. You were put here in this job to lead, do so.

CHAPTER 8

WHAT DO I DO NOW?

So, what do you now? If you made it this far in this book you know that I'm all about leaders learning how to lead. Learning how to lead at the start of their careers, not near the end when it seems like something they should do. Today it's becoming far too common a practice to get promoted through even several layers of an organization before ever once having to make a leadership decision.

Understand that most senior leaders of any company, agency or corporation are going to make mistakes. We are human, and as we know our human DNA will ensure that we don't ever forget that. In some instances, we can learn to control and use that DNA to our benefit. Other times we actually fail at things. In many cases our mistakes are forgivable. Forgivable by our employees and forgivable by the system, the law and our company as a whole. When we make a mistake, it's normally because of pure human nature. We forget things, we are slow to respond to market volatility, but normally it's purely human failure.

Depending on where in your career you are, and at what level of supervision, management or leadership you find yourself; depends on what your next steps should be. If you are just venturing into your first level of supervision, either recently promoted or just looking to see if this is something you really want to do, the answer is easy. If you find yourself well into a career of leading and managing others, it gets a little more complicated. And, if you are that guy or gal who is leading an agency, company, or heaven help you, a government organization; then the answer is exponentially more difficult to answer.

Let's approach these questions in reverse order. As the Chief, the Director, CEO, whatever you call yourself, you most likely are not in the market to relearn, rethink or re-educate what has taken 20 or 30 years to learn. I get it! I do applaud you in getting to this point in a book about accountability. This tells me you do have some desire to better yourself and hopefully more importantly, help your team of subordinates get better while they still have some time left to make a difference in their careers. As the head of an organization, what you say and do still makes a difference in the opinions and careers of everyone below you. Without feeling like you need to make a 180-degree turn in your approach to helping subordinate leaders succeed, a few options are at your disposal.

Start with a simple assignment to your subordinate leaders. Assign a leadership book of your choice as a homework assignment. Now what book are you asking? Well, of course this one is a good start. There are many others, do a little research, it's the least you can do for them.

Give them plenty of time, but not too much time to read it. You, yourself then must also be familiar enough to have some intelligent knowledge of it. I suggest, at your next leadership staff meeting after the reading is done, simply discuss a few chapters. You could even assign subordinate leaders to take on "leading" discussions of specific chapters. Just make sure you give them enough heads up to prepare sufficiently.

With that said, it would be of much greater impact if you led these discussions, but we are going on the pretense that you are not wanting to. That's ok, just the fact that you have asked them to come together and read the same leadership book means you are setting the tone to building a more cohesive team.

This is just one easy suggestion to kick start the learning of your younger supervisors and managers.

There are certainly a variety of other ways to begin helping your subordinate managers. Conduct a leadership offsite. Bring in leadership experts to address your team and allow them to provide some input and feedback. Allow your team to have some down time together (offsite) where they can get to know each other better, on a personal level. It doesn't have to be soft guitar music and smore's around the campfire but when your team better understands the personality of those they are supposed to be working with, they will better learn to work together. All of these are fairly easy to carry out when you lead the agency. Get your Human Resource staff or Training Division on task and set them to it.

Ok, let's move on to the mid-level manager. Maybe you're second line supervisor or district manager. Your job is to keep a host of first-line and maybe some second-line supervisors on task and producing. Producing whatever it is your organization produces. Product, services, widgets you name it. Your job is like that of a circus juggler. You're not so much interested or bogged down by the issues of the line-level workforce, but that of their managers. One thing that this level of leadership almost always involves is personnel management.

At this level, you are designated as the company hatchet-man should it come to that. You will need to be extremely well versed in labor law, personnel actions, hiring and termination processes and staff management. This is a time in your career where the sooner you take it upon yourself to become educated in the ways of managing the process of managing people, the better off you will be.

I will also add that at this level, you should be able to easily build and defend an operations budget. Be able to predict your branch or division's expenditures one or two years in advance.

Travel costs, product or material acquisition, salary and benefits, incidental costs, insurance, and so on and so on. This is your time to learn, live and experience in a micro-way the macro-view of the entire organization. Remember you are only on the hook for your division or section that is but one portion of the company. At some point in your future, should you find yourself promoted up; you will have to begin to combine your knowledge base to expand well beyond this small conglomerate of line-level sections. So, learn it now is what I'm saying! There won't be time or opportunity to learn it later.

But how do you continue to learn and grow as a leader on top of the technical pieces of management? Remember early on in this book when I talked about leaders learning from the past and stepping up today? Where technology has replaced a great many things, but it hasn't replaced good ole' fashioned hard work. Use your technology to learn. Technology is something that your generation (yes, I said it) has grown up with. It's second nature to your world and it should be your go-to when it comes to learning. Learn how to use technology to be a better manager. Understand the variety of software programs in use today. Know what your subordinates are doing and experiencing and manage them accordingly.

As a mid-level manager, you will be expected to increase your learning capacity; not slide into a senior leader position because you deserve it based on time. Now is your time to increase your ability to expand the organization's productivity. You have been at it long enough to know it inside and out, it's up to you to create the next greatest product, the next new widget. If not you, then whom? Most likely it won't be a new, young supervisor, they have enough on their plate dealing with people issues.

The executive level is certainly not going to create the next generation of product lines. It's on you, now's your time. How you do that depends on you.

Finally, let's talk about the first line supervisor, or maybe the up and coming emerging leader that is rising through the ranks and showing great promise. What is expected of him or her to prepare for a promotion to the first level supervisor job? As we've already talked about a little bit, in my opinion this is the most critical point in a person's climb up the leadership ladder.

What is or isn't learned at this early stage of a person's career progression will determine how well they are able to handle critical situations later in their career. This is the time when getting into a basic leadership course is most critical to ensuring a career long understanding of just the basics. Understanding some basic do's and don'ts in how you address your employees, meaning how you communicate with them, both when and where. Work assignments, understanding your roll in their work schedules and how to be fair and equitable, and legal! Dealing with personal issues of your employees, because you will at some point. In short, learning the three principles of leaders; Authority=Action=Accountability as your guideposts can very much determine your success or failure early on.

Learn, learn, learn...read everything you can on leadership basics. Do your research, see what other people saw as mistakes and how they overcame them. Another good option is to reach out and find a leadership mentor. Someone that is not in your branch or division, not in your chain of command, but separate and away from your normal work team. This gives you a better chance to learn about leadership and not more about the business. Right now, you need to learn leadership basics.

A first line supervisor is one of the hardest jobs in the company, but it can also be one of the most rewarding.

Your job in this new position is now not so much about selling, buying, or producing, but about leading people. When you begin to transition to leading people, you begin to start taking on not only the team's issues, but the issues of every person that reports to you. You will find that many times you will become the wife/mother/father/grandfather type figure while at work. Problems they have, become problems you have and that entails helping them through them. When employees are struggling in some other part of their life, their work production and ability suffers. Fix the problem, fix the work issue. It just happens at this level.

Earlier I spoke about how good leaders get to know their team. They know where they come from, the names of their wife and kids, husbands and even when new kids or grandkids come along. Knowing just a little bit about an employee's personal life is about creating relationships, not stalking! Some employees will openly share such information when they feel welcomed and know that your intentions are true and with integrity.

I'm not talking about becoming best friends with your subordinates, I'm talking about having a relationship with someone that you need to be healthy, happy, active and productive while at work. An employee that knows their supervisor understands them a little bit, knows a little about what issues they face at home or with kids, will be supportive when things get strained. Good first line supervisors have to juggle a lot of balls in the air all at once. Their employees, their productivity at work, schedules and vacation time, as well as the bigger branch or division requirements from above. As I said, it can be the best job in the organization while being the busiest one as well.

This is a point where knowing the total array of your authority in this position is so critical!

Know what your options are in dealing with your team right now, today, when you need to be decisive and take action like a first line supervisor should. Learning on the fly is not the way to do it, but it's probably 90% of the way the world does it. Be different, learn it before you are in bad position with an employee. You will be years ahead of your peer supervisors.

In 2019 I created a program for both new and even old leaders alike. It is called "Creating New Leaders Program" and it's a two-day program where we encourage the cohorts to explore their current understanding and assumptions about management and leadership. They will review theories of leadership and better understand the impact leaders make on an organization. As organizations change, so must the need for how leaders; lead. Social interaction, relationships, dialogue and employee accountability matter more today than ever. This course is designed for the new emerging leader as we address some very basic leadership 101 issues, but it has proven to be extremely well received by mid-level managers that have said things like "I wish I had learned all of this when I was first promoted."

That quote alone sums up what I hope will be a lifetime of learning for you, wherever you find yourself today. Whether you bring this program into your organization or find yourself sitting through this course at some point in your future or find another one in your local area. Get into a basic leadership course early in your career. If you can do so before you are ready to be promoted that is even better.

Remember the Navy example that required a basic course of instruction on leadership before you were even allowed to compete? Use that as a guidepost. Learn before you need the information.

As you set out on your career ladder promotions and begin to take on more and more responsibilities keep the three principles of leadership close at hand. Print them off, tape them on your monitor screen, put them where you can see them every day. Authority=Action=Accountability sums up three basic leadership concepts that every leader, regardless of level, can implement and most importantly teach every generation of subordinates below them.

From that evening in the East Room of the White House when the smallest lady in the room took a stand for something she believed in and made a leadership statement. She stood for the principles of having and knowing her authority, taking appropriate action and holding someone accountable (changing behavior) all within 30 seconds. A lesson well learned, and a lesson now passed on.

Do you have the same moxie that Nancy Reagan had that night in the White House? Do you have the same knowledge and ability to lead when you may be the smallest person in the room? Have you discovered your positional authority and learned the skills to confront people you may otherwise be afraid of? Or are you still trying to figure it all out?

Keep reading, keep learning, keep practicing your leadership skills at every opportunity you have. You don't need thousands of people under you; start at home, start at church, start in your community. Practice your leadership skills, practice the three A's and become proficient.

Your organization will recognize your competence as a leader, and you will rise to the top. You can individually turn the tide of being accountable in an unaccountable world.

Connect with Matthew Brandt on Social Media

- LinkedIn.com/in/matthewbrandt1721
- Twitter.com/PolishTheBadge
- Facebook.com/AccountabilityCop/

Contact Matthew at: Matthew@AccountabilityCop.com

Website:

www.AccountabilityCop.com

He would love to hear from you!